CONQUERING
CO-PARENTING

Overcoming Chaos and Stress
While Sharing Custody

Aleka Melson

Published By: Pen Legacy®
Cover By: Christian Cuan
Edited By: Abigail Summer
Formatting & Typesetting By: Junnita Jackson

The author has tried to recreate events, locales and conversations from my memories of them. In order to maintain their anonymity in some instances, the author have changed the names of individuals and places, the author may have changed some identifying characteristics and details such as physical properties, occupations and places of residence.

Library of Congress Cataloging – in- Publication Data has been applied for.

ISBN: 978-1-7354580-8-3
PRINTED IN THE UNITED STATES OF AMERICA.

Table of Contents

FOREWORD

When I first met Aleka, she was a single mother of her two-year-old daughter, Jermari. Although she was facing many of the challenges that were common with being a single parent, her overwhelming commitment was to be the best mother she could be. Aleka's willingness to learn was one quality that has always impressed me. Although there were extremely limited co-parenting resources at the time, she took each lesson in stride and learned daily. Through the mistakes and frustrations, she continued to stay focused on her goal of providing a healthy environment for her daughter.

For over sixteen years of knowing her, Aleka has also demonstrated a commitment to other children and youth. Hence, providing this resource for parents demonstrates that commitment.

Today, co-parenting is a common dynamic in many communities. By offering insight into her co-parenting journey, her wisdom will benefit the entire family for generations to come.

-Jay Cameron

Entrepreneur/ Philanthropist/ Community Leader

APPLAUDS FOR ALEKA MELSON

Aleka Melson came into our lives as a mother in my girl's mentoring program called "I Love Me". What instantly connected our spirits was her commitment to making sure that her daughter, Jermari, participated in every meeting, event, or assignment. She didn't just do a "drop off" but often stayed and provided valuable input for our sessions. She would also volunteer to bring meals for our meetings that were above and beyond the typical pizza and chips. Her meals were in high demand. This is only a small glimpse of seeing and knowing who Aleka truly is. My program was struggling to find and keep strong, committed mentors. So, I asked for help and she immediately volunteered. All I can say is wow! She has been nothing short of a blessing to me, the young ladies, and our entire program.

Proverbs 22:6 says "Train up a child in the way that he should go." Aleka is a walking example of a strong mother, always standing in the gap for her daughter and many others. I admire her strength, faith walk, and willingness to be vulnerable enough to share her struggles with the world. I know this book will be a blessing to those with similar co-parenting challenges.

Thank you for heeding His call and walking in your gift. Tashi Deley!

-Darcel Collins

Founder of "I Love Me" Girl's Mentoring Program

www.fuel4newlife.org

As my dear friend and author, Aleka Melson prepares to launch the inaugural volume of what I'm positive will be the first of many projects in a series of co-parenting guides and materials. I am honored to support her efforts. Having known Aleka for over 35 years, it goes without saying I know her extremely well and we've experienced a myriad of life experiences together. Undoubtedly, her roller coaster of a journey in co-parenting has been the most prevalent and life permeating of them all. Looking back, I can honestly say I've been a participant, spectator, ally, advocate, or witness of a multitude of events, incidents, and occurrences. Through it all, and even during times of extreme frustration, Aleka has always attempted to maintain a level head, a focus on doing the right thing and a posture of faithfulness in God to intercede on her behalf where she stood in need.

Aleka Melson is an intelligent, creative, funny, giving, loyal, and thoughtful woman. What Aleka elects to do, she does with her whole heart and soul. She doesn't stop until the job is complete, and most importantly, she completes them well. This was the same approach and energy she demonstrated in raising and co-parenting her beautiful daughter. Unfortunately, while Aleka was committed to these values and manner of co-parenting, the assumption of fair reciprocation was definitely not a given from the other side. In Aleka's case, not only was reciprocity and cohesion not an assumption to be lightly made, what she experienced was oftentimes the complete opposite of what she was committed to demonstrating.

In theory, the word, co-parenting, might conjure up the idea of parenting together. However, as one half of a "so-called co-parenting team," Aleka's experience has been far from a cohesive team experience. Her participation on the team has many times been riddled with criticism, judgment, false accusations, unfair and unequal expectations, broken court order agreements, and frequent, untrue assassinations of her character. I must admit it could be extremely frustrating to watch someone you love being mistreated and disregarded on such a regular basis. It was evident at times, and Aleka honestly admits that to avoid additional conflict, retaliation, and stress, she became adept at ignoring and avoiding those areas which stood to cause the most stress and perhaps, more conflict. As one might imagine, co-parenting under these conditions was extremely difficult. It was during these times that I would remind her of the many colorful, sparkling, and priceless jewels that would adorn her crown in Heaven. Each jewel, a symbolic representation of what she faithfully endured on her earthly journey in co-parenting. To tell the truth, Aleka's crown will be totally "blinged" out from these experiences alone, not to mention the various ways in which she has been a fine example of motherhood, womanhood, a mentor, and a blessing to others. Thankfully, this thought always seemed to make her laugh and lift her spirits, allowing her to refocus her energy and strengthen her faith in HIS purpose. Her experiences have brought her full circle and her test has become her testimony!

-Kellie Jamison

INTRODUCTION

Oh, the joys of becoming a parent. For many, it's one of life's greatest joys. Undeniably, it was the same for me too. I used to dream of becoming a parent and being the best I could be at it. Most people that plan to have kids in the future generally have an idea of how they want to raise them and how they will map out the steps for each child's success. Even when we have kids that aren't necessarily planned, it's all too common for a new parent to have big dreams for the success of raising a child. We either plan to provide a life similar to our own upbringing or develop ways for our kids to have more than we had. Growing up, I longed to have a traditional family that would consist of a husband with one or two kids. My preference was to have one girl and one boy. As I grew older, I wanted nothing but girls. However, by the time I was a married woman, it no longer mattered what gender I would be blessed with. I just wanted healthy children to raise within a wonderful family. I know I'm not alone with continually having the desired thoughts, dreams, and often a stronger desire to afford each child an equal or better life than what we may have had. What we often don't realize during our "dream thoughts" is that every child is born into this world with an individual purpose. We eventually realize that as much as we plan and prepare, life doesn't always go our way once a child enters our world.

I am blessed to have a daughter and to be a mother. Although I was still married at the time, she was conceived and born while her dad and I were separated. During my pregnancy, I thought I was preparing for the impending co-parenting relationship and assumed that things would all run smoothly. Despite not being together, I felt that we both were ready to love and raise her with nothing but plans of success. I never "really" thought about the fact that my child would be raised in two different households and what all that would entail. I assumed that we'd both be on the same page in raising her, and I just never thought that things could become complicated, difficult, and downright chaotic. Did I even know what co-parenting truly meant? I was so engaged in the excitement of becoming a new mom and at the time, her dad and I got along pretty good even though we were separated. Throw in the fact that I had previously suffered pregnancy losses. I had an ectopic pregnancy and delivered stillborn twin girls during the great times of our marriage. Surely, this blessing on the way will be equally welcomed and loved with no concerns. Shouldn't everything just fall right into place if this child has two loving parents? We were both devoted Christians that were active in the church. Isn't this a perfect foundation for raising a child?

Once our daughter was born, there were things to now consider, such as child support, custody, and visitation. I assumed that we'd work everything out while keeping her away from the court systems. However, her father insisted that the courts must be involved. Just like that, my life became a whirlwind of confusion that led to years of chaos. My personal journey in co-parenting has been challenging to say the least, and at times, it was extremely difficult. As our daughter grew into different phases of her life, the chaos remained with us. It began to have a horrible effect on her. I had consistent moments of frustration and often felt alone in this journey. But throughout the years, as I began to engage with other parents during school events and extra-curricular activities, I began to see that a lot of other parents, both mothers, and fathers, were dealing with some of the difficulties I encountered, in all attempts at having a healthy co-parenting relationship. Chaotic co-parenting was a common thing with parents that had kids in two separate households. I use the word "chaotic" to demonstrate the extreme level of difficulty that I went through as well as other parenting relationships. I began engaging in conversations with both mothers and fathers on this topic, whether they were the custodial parent or not. I encountered some situations worse than mine, while some stated that they started rocky but came to a common ground of peace. I also learned that there were also many co-parenting relationships that worked out great for others from the very start. This book will encompass every scenario from the good, to the bad, and to the never-ending troubled relationships much like mine. I began to speak with several people who gave me advice on how they worked to resolve the chaos even before it went out of control. My goal was to get to a place of peace and continue to raise a healthy child. I wanted this so bad for my own situation and was determined to create ways to obtain this goal. I knew that for this to happen, each party would have to be willing to come to terms with each other, set aside unnecessary feelings about each other, and learn to develop a common ground where everyone could coexist in a positive manner. Then a child will be afforded a healthier lifestyle while growing up within two separate households.

I write this book because I have a passion for our youth. With mental health on the rise, attacking our young people at alarming younger ages, I felt it necessary to develop a tool for parents to use if they find themselves in situations that are affecting their child/children. The last thing anyone wants is to be a reason for contributing negatively towards the mind of a child. Although my co-parenting journey involved years of constant conflict, I had to develop ways to ease the effects it was having on our daughter. After trying different ways to ease the tension and develop ways to be on one accord, it became apparent that I was the only one seeking a resolution to the continuous conflict. I had to eventually develop ways to combat the negative impact it was having on our child. Although I'm not an expert on this subject matter in any form or fashion, I write this book to show examples of my journey as well as others on how chaotic co-parenting can destructively affect a child, and ways to avoid it by sharing examples of great co-parenting situations. I am not an expert in raising a child and was not the perfect parent. Absolutely not! Did I play my part in contributing to the chaos? I most certainly did. But for the fact that I have a heart for our youth and passion for the success of young people, I hope that this book will serve as a resource for someone that may be currently in a similar situation or a guide on ways to avoid the negative impact. As I mentioned, I included stories and examples of great co-parenting relationships from people I've met through the years that were willing to share great advice and tips on how they arrived and were able to maintain healthiness in raising kids. This is not a one-sided guide that is geared towards any particular gender or parenting situation. I recognize that children are raised in many different home environments and are far too many blended family circumstances to focus on one specific home lifestyle.

No matter what state your co-parenting relationship is in, there is hope and ways to conquer and overcome the difficulties that can ultimately lead to a healthy well-loved and loving child. I'm a witness because, considering everything I went through, I found ways to get my child mentally healthy and healed. My daughter, who is now 18 years of age, has become such a well-loved and loving individual towards and from both parents. It doesn't matter if you are a mother reading this or a father reading this. It doesn't matter if you are the custodial parent or the non-custodial parent. It doesn't matter if you have full custody, shared custody, or even live in another state from the other parent. It doesn't even matter if you're the only one providing financially for your child. It takes work to produce a healthy-minded child. It takes us as adults to figure some things out and get a grip on our individual role and not try to play both parent roles when we don't have to. We must come to realize that it's okay to disagree or disapprove when the other parent has a different view on raising a child. You should be responsible enough to learn how to participate positively in your position as a parent. We already live in a world where children are faced with so many adversaries within the school systems, neighborhoods, and communities. Not to mention the effects of social media, which will be discussed in this guide as well. Children are busy trying to discover themselves as individuals, so the home should be where every child should feel safe and well-loved. So, if you are a parent or know a parent that is struggling with a challenging co-parenting relationship, take some time to check yourself first, then set out a plan with determination to develop healthy and positive ways to keep your child winning and successful. That should be every parent's ultimate goal!!!

Several months ago, I had the honor and privilege to attend a "write your story" workshop hosted and facilitated by actress and comedian, Kim Coles. Then, I enrolled in a course she offered afterwards, where I had the opportunity to have a small group meeting by way of the Zoom app and then a one-on-one phone session with her. Although the call was only about 30 minutes, she shared so much wisdom and knowledge and gave phenomenal advice in writing a story. She often referred to us sometimes having to tell the "yummy and yucky" parts of a story and that it's okay to do so. So, what you get out of this book will be some of my own personal "yummy" stories as well as the "yucky" and the stories of others. But I pray that you count it all joy as this is not a book to focus on stories to provoke negative emotions but to possibly see yourself or someone you may know that may need to hear certain aspects of someone's experience in order to grow and be a better person. I ask that you go about reading with a "no judgement zone" mindset, as we are all human and can make mistakes we should learn from.

One last major point before I begin sharing my experience on how I was able to get beyond some of the most trying times of my entire life: Prayer and my relationship with God. Regardless of what you believe in, I just know that I can't imagine how my daughter would've turned out had it not been for the grace of God. My spiritual connection was tested and disconnected several times during this co-parenting experience. There were countless moments where I went astray from surrendering my frustrations, worries, and fears over to the higher power of God. However, once I realized that I could not do this on my own and saw how God was always with me even when I wasn't seeking His wisdom, I knew that prayer, God's grace, and His love were the requisite on how I was able to produce a harvest from all of the seeds He allowed me to sow into raising my daughter. It is my humble prayer that every person struggling with co-parenting relationships taps into your spiritual side and not be led by your flesh. My faith in God was strengthened and ultimately allowed me to arrive at my own peace in the midst of chaotic co-parenting. Some of the chapters in this book may or may not appeal or even apply to you and that is okay. But if you allow some of its substance to penetrate your heart, perhaps, you can save a child from the chaos of co-parenting. Perhaps, you can use this book as a resource to direct someone who may be having a stressful parenting experience. Just have an open heart to receive something that will not only positively affect you, but a child in need of a boost of power in their life. If you are in the midst of a challenging co-parenting relationship, it is my prayer that you seek all of the wisdom, knowledge, and resources to overcome. Many of us have endured and know that through it all, it is possible to OVERCOME!

MY STORY MY TRUTH: HUMBLE BEGINNINGS

When I discovered that I was pregnant, not only was I filled with joy but with fear. I was overcome with fear because my very first pregnancy resulted in having stillborn twin girls. I still remember the vivid details. It all occurred 22 ½ weeks into the pregnancy. I was told to come into my obstetrician's office after I made them aware of a tiny little blood vessel I discovered while using the bathroom. The doctor's office assured me that they believed everything was okay as I could still feel the baby's movement. They requested that I come in only to take necessary precautions. I drove myself to their office with the intention of coming back home afterwards. They immediately pulled me in to do an ultrasound and I remember very clearly as the nurse said, "Well, we know the babies are just fine; just listen to these strong heartbeats." This was music to my ears as I anticipated the doctor to come in. Once my doctor walked in, she reassured me that all was well with the sound of each of the heartbeats I heard through the ultrasound machine. She also did an internal ultrasound to be even more certain. As she inserted the probe, I recall how her facial expression changed a bit. She then used her gloved hand to confirm the look on her face. Her next words were somewhat a blur, but my memory recollects hearing her say, "Mrs. Melson, you have started dilating and it appears that you're leaking amniotic fluid." I can't begin to describe how those blurred words became mixed with confusion on what to say next. What did this even mean for that matter? The doctor continued, "We need to get you over to a high-risk pregnancy specialist immediately for a second opinion." "Wait, what does this mean? What are you saying?" I said, as I tried my best to remain calm. My doctor was very frank and advised that because of the dilation that started, accompanied with the slight leak of the fluid, that I was more than likely going into preterm labor caused by an incompetent cervix. She needed a second opinion to confirm. I was transported over to the high-risk specialist and everything moved quickly from this point on. The high-risk specialist did his examination, then drew me a picture on a piece of what the size of my uterus should look like, which was the size of a small pea. He then drew a picture right next to it illustrating the actual size of my uterus at that moment, which was the size of a grapefruit. He and my doctor concluded that I needed to be admitted immediately for every attempt at stopping the labor process. I was advised that because of the dilation and slow amniotic leak, my life was more in danger than the twins. Although they assured me that they would do everything possible to prevent early delivery, they made it clear that the end result may be having an induced labor to deliver the babies right away. This meant that it was very unlikely chances of survival for the twins at 22 ½ weeks. Once admitted, I was immediately given antibiotics as I rapidly developed a fever. This was expected by the doctors because as they stated, "Because you have started the dilation process, you are open," and infection setting in was almost inevitable. Within several hours, my fever spiked into "danger zone" despite the high doses and different types of antibiotic treatment given to me. By this time, I was surrounded by family. My mother and sister had driven from Maryland to the hospital I was admitted to in Richmond, VA. After about eight hours of praying and waiting patiently, the doctors decided that they would no longer risk it since my life was in danger. They announced that it was imperative to induce labor for an emergency delivery.

Even though I knew at that moment that I was about to deliver twin babies, somehow, I was sure they would more than likely be stillborn. As my doctor made her final assessment and gave me a moment with my family before they began preparations, I remember this unusual calmness that came over me. I was hurting for sure, but it would be an understatement to tell you that I experienced this incredible and unbelievable peace that had never been felt before. My sister was hysterically crying to the doctor to get another opinion as the doctor responded with, "This was the second and final opinion." Everything was moving fast and there was no time to even process what was about to happen but that PEACE!!! It was unexplainable and as the nurse wheeled me into the elevator leading towards labor and delivery, she witnessed me telling my sister, "It's going to be okay. I'm in good hands." The nurse was astonished and literally said to me, "Shouldn't your sister be consoling you instead of you consoling her?" I smiled and said, "God is in control". Even my husband was at a loss for words as tears were uncontrollably falling from his eyes. Once we arrived in labor and delivery, I had to say goodbye to my mom and sister as the nurse explained that this would be a very long process and unfortunately, only me and the father of my unborn children were allowed in the room. They both hugged and kissed me as I again, assured them that I was at peace and in great hands. I knew they thought I was delusional, but all I could express was that I came to a place of total peace. As the inducing began, I delivered one stillborn baby girl and didn't deliver the second baby girl for another 12 hours. This was a long grueling process. Although many tears were shed, I never lost that calming peace.

Our marriage suffered terribly after losing our twin daughters. Four months after the stillbirth, I was pregnant again. However, it was an ectopic pregnancy, as it was discovered early that the fetus was in my fallopian tube and would not produce any viable outcome. These consecutive devastating events caused disharmony beyond repair and eventually led to our separation as a couple. After months of living apart, we began to redevelop our friendship. Then, almost after two years, I discovered I was expecting yet again. Losing our twin girls was absolutely heartbreaking, but I was hopeful that I would not have to endure that anguish again. I was filled with equal amounts of fear as of joy. After making my first appointment with a new obstetrician, I made sure I provided my entire history regarding pregnancy loss. She did an assessment, which included an ultrasound and ordered blood work. She was happy to hear a strong heartbeat at 6 weeks and assured me that she would take every precaution to prevent another loss. She decided to do a cerclage due to my incompetent cervix to prevent preterm labor recurring. According to the medical dictionary, cervical cerclage is known as a cervical stitch, a treatment for cervical incompetence or insufficiency, when the cervix starts to shorten and open too early during pregnancy, thereby causing either a late miscarriage or preterm birth. My doctor informed me that this was necessary to perform in the early stages of the pregnancy. By the 8th week, I have had the outpatient procedure and put on immediate bed rest for the duration of the entire pregnancy since this was considered a high-risk pregnancy. I could not imagine being on bed rest for the total pregnancy and knew this was going to be a difficult journey. Especially, since I lived alone as we were still separated. Yet, I was determined to take every precaution and do everything my doctor advised in order to carry this pregnancy to its full term.

Despite being separated and living in individual households, my husband supported me in every possible way. He would come by every evening and either cook or deliver food. He washed clothes and did various household chores since my bedroom was upstairs in my apartment townhome. Both of our immediate families lived hours away, so he handled his role as "a soon to be father" like a charm. Our friendship remained intact as he held the same concern and compassion for our baby as I did. We never made plans to reconcile and I was content with it. We just eagerly awaited the arrival of our healthy child. Because of our friendship connection, I saw no reason to foresee any drama or issues once the baby arrived; and I never bought it up.

Because my pregnancy was high risk, my delivery was scheduled in which labor would be induced. A week before my delivery date, I was advised that a DNA test would be necessary to make sure he is indeed the father of the child. Thrown completely off-guard, I was confused at the timing and randomness of this announcement. Already riddled with hormones raging from the pregnancy, I kind of snapped back at such an assumed uncertainty. How dare he wait until the week before we welcome a newborn baby girl to have the audacity to question the paternity? What kind of person did he think I was? Wherever the doubt came from, it was now in my face, and although I had absolutely nothing to hide or fear about a DNA test, instead it just imploded my spirit at the thought of him not trusting me. After a heated discussion about this matter; it was diminished and never spoken about anymore. That was until the delivery day.

We arrived at the hospital early on the morning of April 27, 2001. After checking in, the nurses prepped me and began the inducing process. After a few hours, one of the nurses came into my room and said, "I know I've never met you up until this morning, but your husband is an asshole!" Totally caught off guard, I asked how she came to this conclusion. She went on the tell me how he pulled some of the nurses in the waiting area and demanded a DNA test during the delivery. She went on to say he explained that we were in a separated marriage and he wanted to know right away if the baby was his. At this point, I wasn't worried or expressed any form of an emotion projected at the idea of him wanting a DNA test. I was so focused on delivering a healthy baby as I told her to let him do what he needs to do. She further explained that she told him that a DNA test during delivery isn't something that can be done without prior approval and that the hospital would only be focused on bringing a healthy baby into the world. He had no idea that the nurse informed me of his concern, and as he sat with me in the labor and delivery room the entire day, he never made mention it and neither did I. After several long hours of the inducing medication, the doctors discovered that my baby was not dropping down into the birth canal even though I was dilating. They decided to prepare me for an emergency caesarean delivery. Once this process started, everything moved really fast and before you know it, I was in the surgical room with the epidural in place and the delivery process began as he was still right by my side. Within a short period, the doctor's announced, "It's a girl!" Although I had known the sex of the baby during antenatal, it was still such music to my ears. Our daughter was born at 8:11 P.M. as a flood of emotions overtook my entire soul. Emotions of pure happiness as the doctors assured me that she was healthy and weighed in at 7 lbs. and 15 ounces. The moment her dad held her and placed her in my arms, the doctors began talking amongst themselves and quickly whisked my daughter out of my arms as they informed me that they would now have to do emergency surgery on me. During the delivery, they discovered two large cysts on each of my ovaries and they needed to be surgically removed immediately. I could barely understand exactly what was happening at that moment since I was still heavily on medication as a team of doctors rushed over to assist. The procedure didn't take long but felt like an eternity. Once the cysts were removed, the doctors began the stitching process as they advised me of what just occurred. They considered me lucky to have had the caesarean delivery. I, otherwise, would not have known until it became a major complication that could've become a worse situation. I was so thankful for this experience but eagerly awaited my transfer to the recovery room so that I could now hold this beautiful baby God blessed us with.

Two days after delivery, I was still in the hospital experiencing elevated blood pressure levels. The doctors wanted to keep me a few days to monitor my hormonal changes as they worked to bring the numbers down. I had medical providers coming in and out of my room, off and on during the day to perform lab work to observe my progress. I thought nothing of if when a gentleman entered the room one evening with equipment for what I thought was for more routine blood work. He announced to me that he was there to perform the DNA test. Now, my husband was in the room with me at the time and had been there the entire day but had said nothing about setting up this visit. Instantly, I became outraged at the sneak attack that was presenting itself before me. Here I was, in the hospital, basking in my glory of being a new mom, all while fighting elevated blood pressure levels, and this dude said 'NOTHING' about this encounter. The DNA specialist informed me that I was not forced to consent and that I had the right to deny this testing process. Immediately, I told him to proceed with everything that needed to be done to complete the test as I did not have an ounce of any hidden agendas. I allowed this examiner to swab my mouth and that of my newborn, as I held her so gently. She didn't even flinch as I held her in my arms and allowed him to perform the task. My husband was swabbed next and still sat in silence at this entire ordeal. As tears streamed down my face from the hurt felt from this deceit, I couldn't help but wonder how our new role as parents was going to play out. Once the examiner left, I expressed my resentment to him at his gutless attempt to steal my joy. He didn't show much remorse and left shortly afterwards. Later, I learned that his family was behind the demand for the DNA test. Now let's be clear, I don't fault him for one second for requesting the test. We see way too many fathers learning years later that they are not the biological father of their child. Afterall, we'd been separated for over a year before our daughter was even conceived, so I get it. My issue was the deception behind not communicating with me, as well as the overall timing. After everything we'd been through with childbirth, having this test set up behind my back, days after delivering our blessing just did not sit well with me.

I impart all of these details to expound on just how significant it was to finally become a mom. I had gone through a tremendously challenging journey to get to my miracle child and was now blessed with my new role of motherhood. My life was elevated during this time with indescribable joy. I made a promise to God that I would be the best mom I could be and would cherish every moment in this new position. Despite being separated in our marriage that was determined unsalvageable, I was mentally preparing for the joys of parenthood.

THE VALUE OF A VILLAGE

When you first become a parent, you will more than likely often hear the term "It takes a village to raise a child." Some consider it a cliché or just a typical statement that's often heard as we realize that many are involved outside of parents when it comes to raising a child. So, what exactly does this mighty statement really mean? According to various sites on the internet, "It takes a village to raise a child" is an African proverb that means that an entire community of people must interact with children for them to experience and grow in a safe and healthy environment. The villagers lookout for the children." It goes on to say that this does not mean an entire village is responsible for raising a child or the children of a crowd. For me, growing up and hearing this phrase meant a lot different than it did once I became a parent. I already knew that teachers and caregivers play one of the most significant roles in the village when it comes to raising a child. I already knew that family members that step in to assist with childcare and their overall needs are also major roles in the village. But what I didn't realize is that the village can consist of tons of entities that often come into the life of every child at any given moment. Some are there for either a reason, a season, or a lifetime. A "villager" can appear in the form of a coach, a mentor, or even a church leader, just to name a few. A "villager" can be someone you least expect to have an impact on a child. A great village can serve as an outlet for a child at any given age. If you have more than one child, different sources may be needed for each child. It's important to be aware and mindful of who you allow into your child's village. Not everyone that comes along will have your child's best interest.

When I look back over the last 18 years, I realize that my child has been tremendously blessed with the greatest village I could've ever imagined. I further believe that each person was strategically placed in her life at the right time and moment. I can even credit folks becoming part of her village before she was even born. The moment I shared the news that I was pregnant, I had so many people step in to assist during my high-risk pregnancy. As I mentioned previously, I was living in Richmond, Virginia, and away from all of my family. Then, I was a member of a church that I will forever hold near and dear to my heart. When I was placed on bed rest eight weeks into my pregnancy, I didn't even have to ask for assistance. My church family stepped up and assisted me by bringing cooked meals and often bought groceries for me. I even had some accompany me to doctor visits. It was beyond incredible the way they all pitched in to make sure my needs were always taken care of. They even held a huge baby shower for me outside of the other two showers I had from my coworkers and family. Who has three baby showers? I was so blessed to have a multitude of people that genuinely cared and made sure I had everything I needed and more. Once I gave birth, the outpouring of love did not stop. Some assisted me in searching for a childcare provider and to the perfect babysitter. I connected with this childcare provider the moment I met her. Her home daycare was the perfect reference, and it became the perfect fit for my daughter. When I returned to work after eight weeks, I met a young lady on my job that had begun her employment while I was out on maternity leave. She sat next to my cubicle and I found out she had a daughter that was only 3 months older than mine. We connected and she even switched her daughter to my new daycare provider. There were times where we both played tag team for each other as we quickly became friends. If she had to work late, I would pick her daughter along with mine and bring them to my house, and she would do the same for me as well. My village was awesome. Even though I moved from Richmond, Virginia, when my daughter was 17 months, I still kept in touch with her first daycare provider as well as my coworker who I eventually became more like family.

Throughout the years, many have come through and played major and minor parts of our village. Some have even produced lifelong friendships through divine connections, and others served their purpose and moved on. I think about the day at school when my daughter began first grade. I went inside the classroom to meet and greet the teacher and met another mother who was there for the same reason. We were the only two parents that lingered around for a moment as we realized the apparent overcrowding of this particular classroom and we both addressed our concerns to the principal. About a month later, I received a notification that a new first grade teacher had been added to minimize the classroom size. This same mom and I both showed up to meet the new teacher on her first day to ensure that she was a good fit for our girls. I didn't see her again until the next school year as both of our girls were back together in the same class. We connected and kept in touch. At the time, I was a Girl Scout Troop leader and she had an interest in her daughter joining my troop and she did just that. We became lifelong friends. When they were in middle school, she introduced me to a girl's mentor group that her older daughter was a part of, and was now enrolling her daughter that shared the same age as mine. This mentor group changed the course my daughter's life for the better. Had I not allowed the parent connection on that first day of school, I would've missed out on an amazing opportunity for my daughter. This mom became a part of my village and served her purpose that benefited both of our daughters. It had benefits for me as well because after several years, I eventually became a mentor with this amazing group.

Then I think about the time I enrolled my daughter in piano lessons as I was attempting to help her find her gifts. One day, I stumbled upon a simple flyer that had information for in-home piano lessons. I reached out, received a good feel from the teacher, and signed her up. The first meeting was nothing short of amazing, and she instantly connected with my daughter. Although we discovered early on that piano was not something my daughter had an interest in, the bond was formed, and the teacher continued to pour into her life. When I first met this young lady, she was a newlywed with no kids at the time. Her spirit was so profound that we often found ourselves talking long after the lesson had ended. I knew it was a divine connection. She now has three beautiful children of her own and founded a school called "The Living Water School". How amazing is that? We are connected on social media and she is always posting positive things pertaining to her school and personal life, and she continues to be a vessel as I'm able to absorb great knowledge to apply towards my own parenting. She has even come to speak with the ladies of the mentor group that my daughter and I are a part of.

I shared these examples of the importance of defining a village for each child you're blessed to raise. It doesn't mean we have to go out and seek people to be within our village, rather it just shows the necessity of others pouring into our children. As long as you discern in your heart when you stumble upon someone that may be placed in your child's life for a reason, you more than likely will be doing a great thing for your child. As parents, we can only teach but so much to our children, especially when we're not teachers by profession. Of course, we're going to teach based on life lessons, values, and the basics on morals. But it takes a lot more than that. Children require being around others to learn beyond what's taught in each household. We naturally have to monitor who they are subjected to, but we equally need to allow them to learn from the world as we guide and navigate their paths. Each child may require different types of people within their village. Although we live in a world where evilness lies in the darkness to prey on children, we still must allow certain folks in as we use wisdom and discernment. This is because every person that comes within the realm of a child does not always have their best interest. This is where we still have to be the parent and recognize good from evil. As we already know, evil people often come in disguise, and this is why it's utterly important to be involved in every aspect of your child's upbringing. The benefits can be so rewarding for children when they have positive outlets of people that plant good seeds in them.

I once met a young lady that I worked with some years ago. She had two beautiful daughters that were two or three years apart. She was divorced from their father and was struggling in her walk as a single parent. Although the father was somewhat present in the life of their daughters, his presence wasn't enough. The reason it turned out that way was because the mom did not include him in most things that pertained to the girls. So, he didn't make much effort in keeping in touch on a regular basis. When one would get in trouble at school or would get caught up hanging with the wrong crowd, the mom would become so frustrated but wouldn't take adequate action in resolving some of the issues. Venting was her primary form of action. She had a very close-knit family but would never share some of the things that were spinning out of control while she raised her kids. She would hesitantly share with me, only because we had known each other for quite a while. I would often suggest that she reach out to her mom and dad who would probably add that extra needed support, but she always felt ashamed at some of the behaviors her girls were demonstrating. I would suggest placing them in extracurricular activities to give them an outlet and opportunity to build bonds with other peers. I would express the need to have a village to support her in her overall parenting. But through all of my recommendations, she often would shoot them down and attempt to handle everything all by herself. It made things much harder on her as she continued to keep things bottled up between her four walls, and would only reach out to me when things were seemingly getting out of control. The girls are currently in high school and are doing alright academically. But socially, they were both suffering. I would often hear from others of the social media posts they made, apparently screaming for help. Every time I heard it or saw for myself, I would let her know and her frustrations would grow and eventually fade away without resolution. But I didn't stop. Every change I had to speak to her about, I stressed the importance of a village and how a village isn't the right place to tell all of your business or bear your problems to the world. Having a strong village behind every child is just as important as having strong parents. She did eventually place them both in counseling, but only for a short while. She felt it no need to return once she felt they were back to good standings. In my humble opinion, I felt like she didn't know how to help her children through their struggles because she was avoiding her own insecurities regarding her past struggles. I told her this many times and she actually agreed. I continued to pray for her and her children, and I would reach out often to keep sowing seeds. I once read, "We cannot force someone to hear a message they are not ready to receive, but we must never underestimate the power of planting a seed." Sometimes inviting others in as part of our village will help us just as much as it helps our kids. I know firsthand how all of the people in the village for my daughter has truly blessed me. I learn things right along with my daughter.

One of the greatest choices I made for my child was putting her in counseling. She was transitioning from middle school to high school, and as a growing teenage girl, her hormones were flourishing too. She was "smelling herself" as our parents used to say. At the same time, she was having a really difficult time with her dad. She felt as though everything she sought out to do was a disappointment to him. She often felt judged based on her grades and never as a person. Although she wasn't spinning out of control, I knew that if I didn't take some form of action, she would head towards destruction. At the very right moment in talking with a friend who had already been a part of my village, she recommended a therapist the had recently met and felt she would be a good fit for my daughter. I called, made the appointment, and showed up with my daughter on the scheduled visit. The connection with this therapist towards my daughter and I was instant. She sat us down, asked a few questions, and sought out a game plan to work with us. She made it apparent that she was gifted at what she does, and I couldn't have been more please at how God placed her in our lives. She had kids of her own and personal experience with co-parenting and blended families. I expressed that my ultimate goal and intentions were to have my daughter develop a stronger relationship with her dad on her own without my interference. I also laid all of my issues and mistakes that I'd made up until this point and vowed to do much better in reacting to the negative noise that was being lashed towards me. She articulated very clearly; her expectations and her desire to have her dad involved throughout the entire counseling process, but she would do so in stages. There were times where she would meet with me and my daughter. There were times she would meet with just my daughter. The plan was to bring her dad in after several sessions, but she needed him to be made aware right away that our daughter was under her care as her patient. I immediately reached out to her dad to let him know of this game plan. He was a bit apprehensive because he didn't feel the need for our daughter to seek therapy, yet he obliged as I gave him the contact information to introduce himself to this counselor and he did so right away. Once he contacted her, he felt it of utter importance to know every bit of her intentions and requested her credentials. She willingly gave him all of the requested information. After speaking with her, he called me to discuss and asked if she was a friend of mine. I assured him that I had just met her. After several sessions, the therapist reached out and arranged his visit with her and our daughter. Everything went exceptionally well as her dad was on board with helping our daughter with her inner struggles and building a stronger bond between them. However, he never showed up again and ignored all communications when this therapist reached out to him. I'm not sure if he was not ready to allow her within our daughter's village but she was an intricate part moving forward. When I reached out to him to determine why he cut off communication with the therapist, his only response was that he felt like this was a friend of mine and wasn't sure he trusted her. Although it was a disappointment to our daughter, we continued with therapy and she continued to grow through her issues. I never looked back with regret because as time progressed, I watched our daughter grow into this beautiful amazing person. I knew that choosing this person to be a part of our village was worth every single session.

Deciding if therapy is a necessity within your child's village is completely your choice. Although therapy is being sought more and more in our society, some still see it as this "taboo" that's not necessary. Maybe therapy isn't what your child needs. But your child does deserve a strong village. No matter the size of all of those you allow within your circle, it can certainly make a great enhancement to a child's growth. I could go on and on about the countless number of people that have served and continued to be a part of our village. Some were only a part for a short while and some remained to this day. Just consider your options as you carefully allow those in and filter out those that don't always have your child's best interest at heart. If you find that someone is not good for your child, release them and keep moving forward. Just know that a village aids in avoiding steps towards the destruction of a child. A village is not guaranteed to keep a child from destruction, but with the right seeds planted, it surely can do better than not. It is equally rewarding to be a village for a child. Whether you meet them by chance or circumstance, consider being a role model for someone that you're able to connect with. Being a mentor myself, and a coach for my former high school's flag team has been beyond gratifying, and it has taught me so much about myself as a person as well as a parent. Just consider having an open mind when pondering on the value of a village to surround a child.

MIRROR CHECK: LESSONS AND LEARNING

What are your takeaways from this chapter? Does your child have a strong village standing behind them? Do you even agree that it takes a village to raise a child? It's okay to disagree and if you do, I suggest that you check your heart to determine why. Determine if you are one that feels you can raise a child all on your own, with or without the other parent. Check your motives to be sure that you don't view the need for a strong village to be one of selfishness, control, or just overall egotistical. Perhaps, your village is solid for your child. Consider being a "villager" to someone else. I'll leave this chapter with another African Proverb:

"The child who is not embraced by the village will burn it down to feel its warmth."

COURTS AND CUSTODY AND CHAOS – OH MY

Most co-parenting relationships at some point resort to the court systems to help navigate the best interest of the child. Every state has its own regulations and bylaws when it comes to child support, establishing custody, and visitation orders. It can be an overwhelming process when allowing someone of authority, who doesn't know either party to make decisions on your child's behalf. Parents are often on good terms with each other until the courts become involved, and when they are already in cahoots with one another, the court system can make things even worse. But more often than not, the courts are necessary to gain knowledge of parental rights and to establish monetary determinations and residential schedules. It's also important in navigating the fundamentals of every aspect of parenting that we often don't realize that needs to be addressed. There are so many things to consider with a child and the endless circumstances and components that make up the dynamics of a family situation. Oftentimes, legal counsel is brought into the equation to act on behalf of each parent, one parent, or sometimes, just the child. Even more often, children get caught in the crossfire of a parent's desire to want things to be a specific way. Selfishness, bitterness, and all kinds of negative emotions can develop if one is not careful in seeking the best interest of the child. Researching every aspect of desired arrangements and rights prior to submitting paperwork is critical. Otherwise, you could very well walk into a courthouse completely blind-sighted and come out with a result that doesn't necessarily work for you, which certainly won't work for the child either. Knowledge and awareness of parental rights, laws, and everything that comes with the court system will aid in making wise decisions for your parental relationship. It is very easy to get caught up in our feelings when it comes to sharing custody. When a child lives primarily with one particular parent the majority of the time, we feel some kind of way about having to split time with the other parent. The non-custodial parent often feels slighted when they aren't able to see their own child for equal amounts of time or as they wish to. It's certainly not an easy process for anyone involved. Especially, if the situation shifts from an entire family living under one roof to needing to sever the parental relationship due to separation, divorce, or just no longer wanting to be together. It's stressful, painful, and brings forth a whirlwind of emotions on each person involved. More often, the child suffers while the parents seek to figure out and determine the new normal. Holidays, weekends, summer breaks, and birthdays, just to name a few; are things to consider that can be all thrown in the mix of making decisions.   Not to mention the economic aspect in determining financial orders and seeking legal counsel. One can be lawyered up, properly planned, and still walk inside of a courthouse and be stripped of certain components of their child's life. They are all decided by a judge, who has been listening and making decisions on likewise cases all day every day. Judges aren't always concerned about the specific details you present to them. I've heard of judges that make decisions based on their mood for the day. It happens and quite often. I've also heard of judges that will lean more towards a high paid attorney represented parent that is going up against a parent who chose for whatever reason, not to seek legal counsel. The scenarios are endless, yet the court's ultimate purpose is supposed to be in favor of a child's best interest.

I commend families that navigate co-parenting without the court's involvement. I've met many individuals that leave out the stress of a court system that's designed to please everyone.   One must realize that once it's decided to bring the court system into deciding any aspect of your co-parenting situation, things can and will probably shift in ways you can't imagine. I have a male college classmate that I've stayed connected with on social media. Let's call him brother Lee. I say "brother" because his amazing spirit on and off of social media is so profound when he speaks about his son, his son's mother, and their amazing co-parenting relationship. I reached out to him to get some insight as he willingly gave consent to share his story and views on co-parenting. He was once married and decided to divorce when their son was 6 months old.   At the time, both he and the ex-wife resided in Baltimore, MD. During the separation period and prior to the official divorce, brother Lee would have their son to himself 3 to 4 times per week and they alternated this schedule until the divorce was facilitated. Once the divorce was official, they established joint custody and continued with the visitation set up until brother Lee took a job in Washington, DC. Although the distance wasn't much of a difference, it did change where he would get their son on weekends or every other weekend because of school. They maintained and alternated their schedule for major holidays and breaks. He stated, "We actually used to always spend Christmas morning together as a family unit so that he could experience his first part of Christmas with both his parents and no one else around." He went on the explain how summer and spring breaks were arranged, but ultimately, he and his ex-wife did not mind shifting schedules and arrangements when needed. They kept the focus on the child. He also went further with how a few years ago, the mom and son moved to Alabama and he did not object her decision, but stayed connected to their son using more creative ways to communicate. He said that they never followed the court order and in fact, he has absolutely no clue what it even says. They just make it work where it needs to work. Neither of them refers to the court document whenever he wants to be with his son. They communicate and plan accordingly. He said that his ex-wife has ALWAYS maintained the significance of their son being raised with an active and involved mother AND father. Brother Lee exudes with pride as he states "We have never argued in front of him...EVER! And we always present a unified front (even though we may have some behind the scenes disagreements) ...but in front of him, we stand together!" His advice to anyone struggling with co-parenting is, "Keep the main thing the main thing...THE CHILD! Also, acknowledge that you will have some different approaches to some of the nuances of parenting, but regardless, at the end of the day, you BOTH do what you do for the child out of YOUR love. Never talk negatively about the other parent to the child! Now, you two may cuss each other OUT in private...but keep that between y'all. It's gonna happen...just out of the nature of relationships and human dynamics. But mainly, keep the child FIRST, and don't treat the child like an object or use him/her as a weapon against the other parent. That ultimately hurts the child!" What a powerful piece of advice and wisdom that I honestly wish I had received at the beginning of my co-parenting struggles. So, it is not always necessary to keep the courts involved. All it really takes is a mature mindset from both parents to keep the child as their number one priority.

When our daughter was in preschool, I met a couple that had 2 sons at this childcare provider. They seemingly had the appearance of a family structured in a traditional sense and overall, a typical happy loving family. Shortly after meeting them, it became apparent that they were going through a divorce. Mainly because the wife expressed such. I'll call her Miss Bee. She later shared that they were indeed divorcing, and it was becoming a very ugly situation. We stayed connected on social media and I recently reached out to her just to see how she was doing. She willingly shared her story since she already had 16 years of co-parenting under her belt and things were not always pleasant for them. She also knows the importance of sharing if it would help another family from going through some of the things she experienced. Her sons were 2 and 4 when the marriage ended. They relied on the court system as she stated they had everything detailed into a super thick filed document. From drop off and pick up times; to who will be allowed and not allowed to drop off and pick up. Every holiday was established; even the minor ones. She expressed how she spent thousands of dollars for an attorney to make sure everything was covered and there was no room for adjustments. They decided on joint shared custody, which allowed the boys to spend equal time with both parents. Her ex-husband was to pay child support to her because his salary was a bit more than hers. It was ordered in the beginning that he would pay approximately $600 each month. This angered him and he filed a petition to the courts and managed to reduce the amount to $50 per child each month. It was a tougher situation because he wasn't even willing to pay that amount. He ended up in arrears and eventually had his passport revoked. Because of the rigid documented order, they communicated very little, but when they did, there were many unpleasant conversations. The co-parenting relationship caused major chaos as it became difficult to stay on common ground. The kids were both in private school up until their high school years. Through the years, despite the turmoil, the boys weren't heavily impacted. Allowing adjustments with visitations/residential schedules as they progressed in age and becoming active in various sports and activities was one of the good things that happened to the kids. The oldest son is currently in college and the youngest will graduate high school in 2021. Despite the chaos, these boys are flourishing in life with little to no damage caused by the parental relationship.

In my situation, we relied on the court system from the beginning since we were still separated with no intentions of salvaging our marriage. During the first 6 weeks postpartum, I was settling in my new role and enjoying every moment of learning all of the things it takes in handling a newborn. I was living alone with family over 100 miles away, but I had so many friends and church members that stepped in to fill in the gap. Once the DNA test result was returned, showing that my husband was indeed the father (we were still married, yet separated), it was time to discuss how we would navigate our newfound co-parenting relationship. I actually told him that I would rather keep our daughter away from becoming a statistic of the court system and desired to work something out on our own, both financially and regarding visitation. Much to my surprise, my desire was not even considered as he told me that he would rather have the courts involved just to keep things civil and fair. "HE" filed the paperwork for child support and custody. I was shocked that he resorted to this decision, but I went with it. I had already sought out for childcare when I returned to work. Once our court date arrived, we were directed to mediation to discuss all options. We both submitted proof of salaries, and based on a formula, he was ordered to pay over $900 per month. Suddenly, my child's father rose up with anger and dismay at such a sizeable amount that he was expected to pay. He demanded a reduction and then looked in my direction, inquiring how much I was originally going to seek prior to coming to court. At this point, I felt it unnecessary to disclose that amount I was planning to request; although it was significantly lower. Because I had taken time off from work and waited hours in the courthouse since he didn't want to discuss this amicably without the court system, my deal was off the table. I did oblige and admit that I was only going to ask for $600 per month. But again, my offer was no longer on the table. It had nothing to do with spite but for the simple fact that the mediator was able to break down all of the expenses that occur with a newborn outside of childcare, which I hadn't even considered. He remained furious for the duration of that session and I did settle for a slightly lower amount that was less than $800. When asked regarding custody and visitation, he decided to request liberal visitation. While we both would have joint legal custody (decision-making), I would have full physical custody. At the time, we lived less than 10 minutes away from each other and the reason he did not want to set an allotted time and schedule to spend with his daughter. I agreed with this and therefore, no further issues arose regarding our first court case on visitation and custody. But that was only our "first" encounter with the court. By the time our daughter was almost 2 years old, I decided to move back to my hometown in Maryland. The decision came after I almost lost my job due to the fact I called out of work on several occasions our daughter was sick. Unfortunately, she was a child that had numerous ear infection occurrences and I could never depend on her dad to assist with caring for her when she was ill. Although it was a very tough decision as I did not set out to intentionally move her away from her dad, I deemed it necessary so I could have additional support from my family. He did not attempt to prohibit me from making this move, even though we both knew he would've been within his legal rights to do so. Immediately after relocating, approximately 100 miles away, we made necessary adjustments to the court orders to establish a more rigid visitation schedule. We established the typical "every other weekend" alternating holidays and meeting location and times for "drop off and pick-up" exchanges. It worked for a short while, but moving away from him seemingly triggered adverse reactions in this newly adjusted co-parenting setup.

If I told of how many times we were in and out of court, I'd have another book. Let's just say that as time moved on, I was constantly receiving subpoenas to appear in court regarding custody and visitation adjustments, child support modifications and accusations of court-ordered violations. Things got worse and developed into real chaos the day I received multiple subpoenas all at once; ranging from him requesting full physical custody to accusing me of violating the visitation order. Our daughter was only 3 at the time and has to now be assigned a "guardian ad litem" to act on her behalf. Neither of us had previously used legal counsel, but he did with these new petitions. After taking our daughter to meet this guardian ad litem (a female), she immediately told me that she was not going to recommend that full custody to be granted to our daughter's father because he did not have any grounds for it. She went on to state that he even advised her that I was a great mother, but he wanted our child to be raised by him simply because he just wanted to raise her full-time. At this point, I felt it necessary to seek legal counsel and did so. Once it was known that I had sought an attorney, he did the same and the chaos grew even worse. There were a few continuances requested by our attorneys and this all lasted for several months. All of the petitions were eventually thrown out, other than a few modifications to the visitation schedule. It was a difficult period where anger escalated towards one another simply because we were both immature and weren't keeping focused on the star of the story; our precious daughter. Why weren't we more mature about the nature of our child's wellbeing? Why couldn't we be like "brother Lee"? Looking back, I can say that although we equally loved our child, we weren't loving enough to look past our differences. After many more court orders and attorney involvement on his end, he was able to reduce his monthly child support down to be a little less than $300 per month. Frankly, I was tired of fighting it and I settled for this ridiculous amount for more than 10 years until our daughter turned 18 years old. I say ridiculous because he earned much more than I did, had since remarried and had two additional daughters with his new wife. The judge even encouraged me to petition for an increase every few years due to the increase in the cost of living. I no longer had the fight in me to do so. I could no longer endure the unnecessary drama. I struggled financially through the years but felt it necessary to surrender the court battles to maintain my own peace. Was it fair? Absolutely not!! Especially, when he wasn't even willing to assist with the many extracurricular activity costs or anything outside of a child's daily needs. I managed and grew in the faith that carried me through. Once our daughter became a senior, I reached out via email asking that we set aside any differences that we've had and work together since "senior year" is extremely expensive. I mapped out all expenses that would occur from senior pictures, senior trip, and the overall senior dues package. My plea was responded to with a phone call as he told me that since our daughter had turned down a job he had lined up for her that summer and chose not to come to Richmond for her court-ordered 6-week summer break, he had no intentions of contributing towards anything regarding her senior expenses. He held on to his words and he didn't. I didn't argue with his stand because I knew that our daughter had a mighty village that would step in as they always did and make sure she had everything she needed for her last year at high school.

My story is not a reason for anyone to stop seeking what's fair and just when it comes to a child. Children go through and grow through many ages and stages in life that require court-ordered adjustments. The older they get, their individual lifestyles tend to change and require less rigidness when it comes to following a court document. If parents aren't on the same page when orders require adjustments, it will just keep the chaos going. I was able to grow away from my participation in negative behavior. My boundaries were set, and I continued to do my part as a mother in nurturing our child and stayed focused on producing a well-rounded individual. My only regret is not having the visitation adjusted during the high school years. Our daughter was heavily involved with activities, which often required her to miss scheduled weekends with her dad. He was pretty cooperative in that manner but when she requested to miss a weekend to attend social events with friends, he would not allow any compromise and rejected it outrightly. This caused constant conflict between them and I was often blamed for it. My advice to anyone in any type of tumultuous co-parent situation is to do your part, stay in your lane, and fight fair for your child's best interest. Set the necessary boundaries to prevent you from stepping outside of yourself when you know you're doing everything in a positive manner. Seek legal counsel when necessary and more importantly, maintain your peace. Develop a relationship with God and strengthen your faith. I recently read a powerful quote that resonated with me. It states "To be absent from drama is to be present with peace."

MIRROR CHECK: LESSONS AND LEARNING

What are your takeaways from this chapter? What role do you play when it comes to decisions, custody, the courts, and any chaos? Is the court system a necessity for your family? Are you willing to make necessary adjustments based on the child growing through different stages? If you are walking well in this lane, I commend you but also encourage you to offer advice to anyone you may know that is not handling things well in this area. Be a village by sharing your personal tips for maintaining peace. Also, if you find yourself adding to or being the primary cause of chaos, I recommend that you look in your personal mirror (metaphorically speaking) and check that heart of yours. Check your motives and dig deep to discover ways to create peace. Consider this quote by Doe Zantamataer: "If the plan doesn't work, change the plan but never the goal." The goal should be THE best interest of the child. Not your best interest, but the child. If you find yourself struggling as the only parent willing to make it solely about the child, I encourage prayer.

MANIFESTING YOUR MELTING POT

Perhaps, the title of this chapter has your mind wondering where this could possibly go. Well, because nowadays, children are more often a part of a blended family as it's normalcy in this day and time. According to the internet, "the simple definition of a blended family, also called a stepfamily, reconstituted family, or a complex family, is a family unit where one or both parents have children from a previous relationship, but they have combined to form a new family." There are countless types of family dynamics that make for a blended family and can often be just as chaotic or stressful as dealing with co-parenting issues. Children generally don't have much control when becoming a part of a blended family, and it's therefore important for them to be gently migrated in. I have encountered many friends and family members navigating their own blended families and have often seen some work for the good of a child, and some, not so good. Depending on the age, and sometimes the gender of a child, it's essential in providing a smooth transition for children as they enter and blend with newfound family members to minimize the effects that could arise. Most times, the new family structure is unfamiliar to all within, hence, the title name of this chapter. Change in anything is inevitable and it often requires the mind to shift into whatever position that is before them. Every person within the newly blended family deserves an understanding of all the roles involved but ultimately deserves respect, especially from and towards the child.

Personally, I do not have experience with being in the midst of a blended family, but I can imagine it's not easy for everyone involved. My daughter, however, experienced this transition when her dad remarried. She was 7 years old at the time and had known her new stepmom since she was about 3 or 4 years old. Although I was never formally introduced, we both acknowledged each other by speaking and being cordial whenever we were in each other's presence, which wasn't quite often. I generally have a good sense of judgement when it comes to a person's character and judging by how highly my daughter spoke of her; I did not need to be concerned. Contrary to what most would think, I trusted my ex-husband enough to know that he wouldn't just allow anyone to enter our daughter's life, let alone become a stepmom to her. There were some adjustments on my end that I had to get used to, especially after they got married. From the time my daughter met her now stepmom, she called her Miss (blank). Immediately after they were married, it was suggested that our daughter call her "mommy." Now, "clutch your pearls" as I surely had to do when I received wind of this. But because I was in a more mature state of mind, I was able to talk this through by asking "What do you feel comfortable calling her"? She stated just as I thought she would. "I have always called her Miss (blank) and don't feel that I should call her mommy." Of course, I didn't like that this was even something I ever thought I'd be discussing with our child, but here we were. We talked about it and swiftly moved on from that. It never became an issue or was never bought up again. I also never had to hold a conversation with her dad about it. I considered this new family dynamic a bonus for my daughter because her dad and I were already having difficulties navigating our co-parenting relationship. I was not about to enter the arena of interfering with her new role within this blended family. As far as I was concerned, his wife is a pleasant woman and felt she genuinely loved our daughter as her own. For the most part, she never gave me any reason to dislike anything about her. As my daughter got older and was able to articulate a lot more, there were moments of concern where her stepmom would either express something to my daughter or do something that wasn't pleasing in my sight. However, I still maintained peace by not approaching anyone on any of my concerned matters. I would simply communicate openly with my daughter, encouraging her to process everything by embracing her stepmom for who she is. Approaching either of them would only make matters worse. Also, because it was her dad that told her to call her stepmom "mommy," I knew that this was a personal sneak attack towards me. He knew she would tell me. But again, I was so much more progressed in my maturity that I was so unbothered. It reminds me of a quote I read that states "How beautiful is it to stay silent when someone expects you to be enraged". Yes, God!!! That's a word for me!!!! But I digress.

One of the reasons I never interfered with this particular "melting pot" is because I knew my role as a mother and that nothing or no one could ever change that. I was learning to stay in my lane. I also recalled an event I once attended that changed my entire perspective towards stepparents. It was an all lady's prayer event. In the middle of the program, something was said that convicted the heart of a particular woman, which caused her to wail uncontrollably. I mean she wept for what seemed to be an hour, as she experienced a very profound breakthrough that caused everyone in that room to pray for her. She kept calling out her stepdaughter's name and it somewhat spoke thru her cries that she had failed her. Because I was friends with her and she is a woman I admired. I later reached out to her and inquired what that was all about. She hesitantly shared her story with me and permitted me to share in this book as she feels, so her story could be heard. She went on to say that although she felt ashamed and somewhat embarrassed about what she was going to share, stating that if it would help someone else, then she would willingly share her story. She was emotional as she conjured up the memory and the night of her breakthrough, stating that because it was so deeply intense in her heart, she knew that God would want her to share. So, I'll refer to has as Ms. Jane. She had been married for several years and had a son. Prior to marrying her husband, he had a daughter from a previous relationship. She adored this stepdaughter and took on her position as a stepmom like a champion. Ms. Jane grew up with both of her biological parents but had issues of not feeling affirmed by her father and sometimes her mother. There wasn't any affection and encouragement given and this left her to grow into adulthood with deeply rooted insecurities and low self-esteem. Growing up, she lacked confidence and never felt good enough to her parents, especially her father. There wasn't any reassurance and support of her dreams and desires. She never really felt unconditional love that little girls long for from their daddies. This caused her to secretly and inwardly envy the beautiful relationship between her husband and his daughter. She saw her husband showing the unconditional love and adoration that she longed for when she was growing up. This caused her to treat this innocent little girl with a mean spirit. She stated that she would say and do little mean things because she witnessed her husband portray a father's genuine love towards his daughter, which caused her to grow resentment. She knew that these deep-rooted issues were not conducive to who she was supposed to be as a wife, mother, and stepmother. Her heart was convicted to breakthrough and break free of these feelings. The great thing about this situation is that the daughter was so young and wasn't even mature enough to realize and understand what was really going on. From that moment of conviction, Ms. Jane worked to change her heart completely and became a changed woman and grew to love and treat this daughter as her own. They grew to have a beautiful relationship and continue to do so. As Ms. Jane shared this story with tears of shame in her eyes, I assured her that she is awesome for being transparent and we all fall short at times in being our best selves since we are just humans. No one should cast judgement on her because she overcame, turned things around, and grew her heart to be so much bigger than she could've imagined. I have nothing but admiration for her and her family is blessed. As I'm reminded of Proverbs 23:7 "As a man thinketh in his heart, so is he," it is my prayer that she knows her heart has been wiped clean.

Ms. Jane's story convicted my own heart because I knew that my daughter was now part of a blended family and I can't imagine how I would feel if I knew my child was being treated unfairly. It also allowed me to view her stepmom from a different vantage point. They eventually had two daughters and my daughter excelled in her role as a big sister. Their melting pot isn't perfect but it's theirs. No one should expect perfection in blended families because there's no such thing as that, just as there is no such thing of perfection in co-parenting. My daughter is part of this melting pot and I do my part by staying in my lane. For the fact that she goes to counseling with her therapist, she has the necessary tools to keep her flowing in her lane as a daughter, a stepdaughter, and a big sister.

I met a young lady a few years ago that married a gentleman that has a teenage daughter. I'll call her Ms. Dee. Ms. Dee came into the marriage with 2 young daughters from a previous relationship. Her daughter's father also has kids from a previous relationship. So, after your head stops spinning enough to comprehend the total children within this melting pot, just know that the mindset of this entire blended family works amazingly well. Everyone understands their individual role and they all work together to keep this pot stirring with positive things. There are times where Ms. Dee's husband will coordinate visitation drop-offs and pickups. Every single adult person within this melting pot all get along and have nothing but respect for one another. All of the children are free from unhealthy issues that could affect them negatively. They have manifested their melting pot to work for everyone, and that should be commended because it's not a common trait to see. If you are part of a blended family, it is my prayer that you make things work for the simple fact of producing healthy-minded children.

MIRROR CHECK: LESSONS AND LEARNING

What are your takeaways from this chapter? Are you flowing in your lane within your melting pot? Do you have a child or children within a blended family? Is there a moment of reflection that requires a heart check? Perhaps, you already have a good mindset that requires no change. Perhaps, you know of someone that does. Would you be willing to share your good experiences with others if you knew it would help a family manifest into something more beautiful? Every child deserves to grow up in healthy home environments. Regardless of the family dynamics, as adults, it's our responsibility to give every child our very best no matter which lane our role lands in.

BUILD! DON'T BREAK HEARTS

While this chapter talks about daddies with daughters, I hope that you would keep reading even if you feel this doesn't apply to you or your circumstances. You may know someone with a similar story or someone who can relate to this. This chapter articulates times of disbelief for me as I witnessed and experienced events that no little girl should ever have to encounter.

So, let's talk about girls. Our daughters. Sugar and spice, all things nice; that's what little girls are made of. An old wise quote or rhyme that appears in many variations or forms. Little girls are expected to be raised to become healthy young ladies. One of the most heart-wrenching things to witness or hear about is a little girl suffering from a broken heart. Especially, when it's totally unnecessary and preventable, and even more disheartening when it comes from a parent. It's already tough when grown women suffer from broken hearts, but it's another thing to see innocent children walking around with hurt and pain within their little hearts being torn apart. I recently saw the following quote and it made my heart skip a few beats as I recalled a few instances where my own daughter's heart was broken, as well as other young girls where I've witnessed this. I do not know the author of this quote, but it states:

"A lot of fathers broke their daughter's heart long before any man."

Let me first share a story from several years back when I was a Girl Scout Troop leader. I was part of a committee that decided to throw a father/daughter dance for our entire service unit area. I was excited as everyone else on this committee because there's nothing like watching daddies with their little girls. I knew this would be a great event for my daughter with her father since he lives out of state and although has regular visitation; it would serve as a memorable night where they both have a chance to dress formal and dance while projecting a memory to last a lifetime. One of the parents in my particular troop was a good friend of mine. When I first met her several years prior, she was married with two beautiful girls. She eventually got divorced and separated from her husband and was having a difficult time in their own co-parenting relationship. But for the most part, they were seemingly on good terms with each other when it came to their daughters. The father called me up and immediately purchased tickets for him and the girls to attend. He was excited as were the two young girls. At the time, they were probably about 10 and 12 years old. On the day of the event, their father called their mom and asked if he could get dressed at her house and then escort their daughters to the dance. Mom stated she didn't think it was necessary and advised to come and pick them up in time for the dance. This didn't sit well with the dad as he proceeded to tell her that he was no longer going to the dance if he won't be given the chance to get dressed at her house. Now, I was also acquaintances with this father, so when mom called and told me about this conversation, I just knew he wasn't serious and called him myself. Sure enough, he told me the same thing. He ranted on about the mom being selfish and became belligerent about her situation. I begged him not to make this decision since this dance was about the girls and that they were looking forward to it. I didn't have any luck before disconnecting, but I believed in my heart that he would still show up. Especially, since it was still several hours before the start of the dance, and I assumed he would cool down and come to his senses before the time. I arrived early to set up and assist with the entire night. Once our daddies and daughters began to arrive, I realized I hadn't seen this father show up with his daughters yet. An hour after the dance started, the mom called me to the parking lot. She was sitting in the car with the girls who were crying hysterically because their daddy did not show up. It was an unfathomable scene. The mom began to cry along with the girls as they all had called his cell phone and house phone several times with no answer. I even called myself and much to my dismay, he did not answer any of our calls. The mom left and took the girls back home and as she arrived, her next-door neighbor was outside and ran to their distress when he saw the tears. He was an older retired gentleman and offered to be the girl's escort for the night to stand in for their dad. They accepted and his wife made sure he was dressed dapper and distinguished for the occasion. When the three of them walked thru the doors of the dance, I saw all smiles on each face as the girls were happy to now be at the dance. They had a wonderful time despite their dad not showing up. However, the hurt never left their hearts.

Fathers!!!! It is my prayer that if you are reading this, that you would never in a million years bestow this type of pain on your darling daughters. Even if you find yourself in a similar situation, think about the child at all costs. We, as parents, cannot get so engrossed in our feelings that we allow our children to suffer at our expense. This particular example was a total act of selfishness and childishness and will be remembered for a lifetime. Of course, dad apologized to the girls after the act, but this didn't take away the hurt they felt in that moment. Especially, since it shouldn't have happened. Add to the fact that pictures were taken of this formal event, so these memories will always remain with them. I'm just thankful that as time progressed, they were able to forgive their dad.

I recall one of the times when my daughter's heart was broken by her dad. In her first year in middle school, she joined the modeling team and developed a passion for it. Now, remember I mentioned that my daughter struggled with academics since her early elementary years, but was smart, nonetheless. Her transition into middle school was already challenging because this is the pre-teen/teen age where hormones are on the rise and adjustments from elementary to middle school were interesting. The modeling team had a competition coming up and this was her first time competing in an event. So, you could imagine her excitement when she asked her dad to attend. Even more, excitement as he purchased tickets for him and his family, which included her stepmom and two younger sisters. As the time for competition day got closer, she was still struggling with a few classes but nothing out of her usual. I was already involved enough with each teacher to know that although her grades were fluctuating, she was still putting forth an effort. I would always tell her that as long as she is putting her all into studying and doing the best she could, then I was content with that. I watched her study. I studied with her. I watched her do her homework and saw evidence on the school's online system that it was turned in. She was already on a 504 plan that allowed classroom modifications since previous testing indicated that she needed assistance. When competition day was approaching, her dad was not pleased with the grades he saw online and told her that he would not allow her to compete. I expressed my disagreement since I knew and understood her struggle. Her visit to him the week before this competition was riddled with hurt and pain. He sat her down along with his wife as they both said to her, "We don't support children with bad grades and therefore will no longer be attending." Her heart was crushed as she told me this. She said she pleaded with them that she was really doing her very best. They felt it wasn't good enough and stood their ground. Not only were they no longer attending; they requested that she pay them for the tickets they purchased that were not refundable. Yes, you read this correctly. A father is telling this to his 13-year-old child that she has to pay them the $45 they felt were now being wasted since they would not be in attendance. Despite this devastating announcement, she still believed that they would show up since they never gave her the tickets to at least sell them to someone else. The day of the competition arrived and my family came out in numbers to support her. She still had faith that her daddy was coming. At the end of the competition, it was announced that her school won the first place title, something that hadn't been accomplished for years with this school; one can imagine her and the team's excitement. Immediately they were dismissed, she came running off the stage to find me and she jumped into my arms with tears streaming from the accomplishment of winning first place. Her first words were, "Where's my daddy"? I told her that he was not there. She then ran to other family members after she dismissed the reality that he really didn't show up. She was still beaming in the excitement as to be expected. When we proceeded to leave, she said, "My daddy really didn't come". Although highly disappointed, her excitement of this triumph was weighing over this heaviness. She immediately wanted to call him to share the good news and she did. She called during the ride home from her cell phone and when he answered she said, "DADDY, DADDY, GUESS WHAT? OUR TEAM WON FIRST PLACE!" Then there was silence. She proceeded to speak in a lower tone that exemplified the hurt being projected over the phone. Once she disconnected, she began to cry for a moment and then said, "Why is he so mean and harsh towards me?" I asked what he said that drew her to that statement. She told me his exact words were; "Okay, but I still feel you didn't deserve to compete, and you still owe me the $45 for the tickets when you come for your next weekend stay." He refused to offer congratulatory praises or anything remotely close to celebratory words and was still harping on her paying him back. It crushed her spirit but the anger it provoked in me was unfathomable. I really wanted to understand his logic behind his attempt at disciplining her for what he felt that her grades weren't good enough. Nothing in me could come to any common ground with him. I was furious because I knew the work she put in balancing school and extracurricular activity. She never forgot the hurt she felt that night. It was her first heartbreak and it happened to come from her daddy. Months later, when she received money for her birthday, he indeed made her give him his $45. Although their relationship had already had its share of minimal despair, this was very difficult for her middle school mind to wrap around. She had always considered him her hero up until this point, and now I was left to figure out a healthy way to bring her back to a place of loving and trusting her fallen hero, and put the pieces of her heart back together as best as I can.

Before you allow these stories to provoke anger within your own heart, please understand that this is not the purpose of sharing this story. The purpose is to show moments of how unwise decisions or unkind gestures from a parent can heavily affect a child's heart. Despite my own sparked resentment at both situations when it happened, I truly do not feel that it was the ultimate intention of these fathers to cause hurt towards their daughters in either instance. Regarding the story of my girl's scout father; the love and respect he had for his daughters did not outweigh his selfishness at that moment. As humans, we all have weak moments of despair that end up hurting others; especially our loved ones. Regarding my daughter's father, I believe he wanted to be a parent that wanted the best for his daughter and chose to discipline where he saw fit in that moment; all the while not realizing that his gestures would provoke the hurt that it did. I don't for one moment believe that either of these dads set out to deliberately hurt their baby girls. However, I did not arrive at these thoughts at the time it occurred. I had to allow God's grace to show me these things in order to experience some sort of peace.

Ephesians 6:4 New Living Translation (NLT) "Fathers, do not provoke your children to anger by the way you treat them. Rather, bring them up with the discipline and instruction that comes from the Lord."

MIRROR CHECK: LESSONS AND LEARNING

As adults, we need to learn to use our words to effectively communicate. I do not have to raise my voice or even get out of character to prove a point of view. A quote comes to mind that a friend of mine shared on social media that states: "Everyone has the potential to bear good fruit, but your crop gets tainted, pull it, re-plant, re-water, & re-nurture. Please don't poison innocent people." Children are innocent people deserving of love and respect from each parent. If you are a parent or know of a parent that is guilty of provoking pain that ultimately hurts a child, learn from it, grow from it, and help prevent someone from doing the same. It is equally important to address the heartbreak with the child. Help them understand that hurt people are people that haven't healed. When we don't realize we even need healing, we go on with life and the silent hurt builds up and becomes toxic. If we're really being honest and mature about it, we will realize and gain an understanding that we all have some sort of toxic traits within us. Learn to recognize it when it arises and be responsible enough to not ignite these traits into the hearts of a child. ESPECIALLY, when it's your child. Only then will you prevent passing down a trait that could be repeated in other ways when that child becomes an adult.

As quoted by Socrates: "To know thyself is the beginning wisdom."
2 Peter 3:18 New Living Translation (NLT)

Rather, you must grow in the grace and knowledge of our Lord and Savior, Jesus Christ.
All glory to Him, both now and forever! Amen. Hurt

UNNECESSARY NOISE

"Peace. It does not mean to be in a place where there is no noise, trouble, or hard work. It means to be in the midst of those things and still be calm in your heart."
(author unknown)

Have you ever encountered a person that seem to constantly ignite something to argue about or disagree with? Like little things that have absolutely no significance to anything. I see this all too often when observing how some parents interact with each other. I've seen it amongst married couples who are parents as well as single parents. What are we talking about here?

When you are co-parenting, you cannot avoid interacting with each other no matter what. It doesn't matter whether you're on good terms or bad terms with each other. Communication amongst each other is everlasting until the child becomes an adult. It's best to figure out ways to communicate in a positive manner, but it's not always that simple. If the relationship is already in a state of chaos, we tend to react in a negative way towards the one spewing out the initial negativity. Before you know it, both parties are getting nothing accomplished when attempting to relay what needs to be said. Poor communication in co-parenting relationships can do damage to a child. We often assume that it can't have a devastating effect as long as the child is not around during difficult conversations. But once you engage in an unhealthy conversation, it will change your character at that moment, if you absorb the negativity components. Therefore, it can easily spew out into a child by your actions and words if we allow it to consume us. So, let us be honest with ourselves and realize when we get caught up reacting or causing negative conversations.

Communication between my daughter's father and I was pretty rocky for the majority of our parenting years. Most of our conversations went south from the beginning on both sides. We seldom were on one accord when it came to our discussions on anything pertaining to our child. I wanted to be heard and so did he. Neither of us had good listening skills when it came to talking to each other, as it always ends up talking back at each other. There is a difference. In the early years, when he barked, I would bark right back with unkind words just as they were hurled towards me. Then, there were times where I initiated the barking. When I say "bark," it doesn't mean just yelling or talking loud at each other. It could mean a negative tone or sarcasm, and just anything conveyed with the intent of making sure your point was given. Something simple would soon become a big elevation of a mess and often leaving the initial topic unresolved. Even more often, the conversation would take such a turn that we'd forget about what we were discussing in the first place. "Oh, the child; that's right" lol. Once the negativity sets in, it no longer was about the child as anger or resentment now takes its place at the moment. For me, I saw how I would have this adverse undertone when talking to my daughter soon after that had absolutely nothing to do with her. Once I realized that this poor communication was developing into changing my character, I had to figure out a way to cease my participation in this battle and make changes in how I communicated and I allowed myself to be communicated to. It wasn't easy and it came with many failed attempts. My first voice of reasoning was that I could not take things so personal. Most times when we're communicating negatively, it comes from a place of hurt or frustration. I literally had to talk to myself at times before I even engaged in an upcoming conversation. I had to strategize my responses and reactions to stay true to myself and focused on the topic that was presenting itself. Most times, insignificant conversations made out to appear as though it was child-related were not as it seemed. For example, I recall a time when my daughter was still a toddler. At the time, my mom was a consultant for a well-known catalog company called Popular Club. They offered designer merchandise, from clothes to electronics and even major household products. My daughter was her only grandchild and she spoiled her as most grandparents would do. I remember a pair of jeans she gave me for my daughter that was of a very popular designer. This pair of jeans were so cute, and I loved seeing her in them. I packed them in her bag for one of her scheduled visitations with her dad. I later received a call from him, almost instantly yelling about why I would put on expensive designer clothes on a toddler. Although I was a little taken back regarding the subject matter, all I could do was focus on the fact that he was questioning me about what clothes I put on our child. After he fussed about it, I fussed right back. During the argument, I did mention that my mother purchased the jeans but I'm not even sure he heard it or even cared. My thoughts were "How dare you tell me what to clothe my child in?" The summary of the point he was attempting to make was "Why are you wasting money on designer clothes?" Hence, the backstory was him being in his feelings about having to pay so much in child support. Basically, he felt it wasn't right for a toddler to be wearing such expensive clothes. Neither of our points had any value because, at the end of the day, the jeans were purchased (regardless from who), she was wearing them and nothing in that moment could change the facts. Being able to now dig deeper into that particular conversation, I realized that it was just noise and unnecessary commotion. I also realized the underlying reason had a lot to do with control and money. But nonetheless, "TOTALLY" unnecessary. He even took it a step further and demanded that I no longer send clothes when she came to him since he would provide his clothes for her. He specifically wanted the clothes she traveled in and an outfit to return in. "Say what now?" This was completely contradictory to me because, on one hand, you feel like you're paying way too much in child support, but now questioning how I use it. But adding his own wardrobe to keep at his house for her meant that he spent more money on clothes she would only get to wear every other weekend. Not to mention the rapid growth of children, particularly toddlers, where she would only have a chance to wear a few times before she outgrew them. This was an unquestionable waste of a conversation and of my time. But I sure did participate and kept on fussing at how ridiculous this was. Pure unnecessary noise!

Another "once upon a time" of when I was confronted with a pointless conversation was when I found it was time for our daughter to start using deodorant. She was about 7 or 8 years old at the time and I received a call as he wanted to know why I was putting deodorant on her at such a young age. He went on to express that girls don't require deodorant at that age and that I should try changing the type of soap I was using on her. I was still using baby soap products and he knew this. I loved the way these types of soap smell and knew these products have nothing to do with underarm odor. I kept calm in the beginning as I advised him that every child comes into the "deodorant" stage in their own time. There are no manuals to follow to keep body odor at bay. When the hormones arrive, the odor hits when it's supposed to. "Did he think I could control armpit odor?" Needless to say, as immature as this conversation was, I added my 2 cents and more as I let him have it. Why was I getting all "swelled" up about discussing body odor that NEITHER of us had control of? It's because it was noise and I hadn't learned how to "not" react to and ignore it. But let me not seem so one-sided on this subject because I had my share of contacting him on some petty stuff too. I recall a time when I picked my daughter up after a weekend with her dad. She was younger at the time; maybe about 4 or 5. As usual, I asked how her weekend was and what all she did. She mentioned that her daddy took her to one of her favorite places at the time; Chuckie Cheese. She

74

went on to talk in excitement about how much fun she had and every little detail surrounding that outing. Then she mentioned a female's name that accompanied them. Wait. What now? You already know that I was not pleased to hear this with my immature mindset. We had been divorced a few years by then and it was only natural that we were both free to date and see whoever we wanted. But in my mind, I'm thinking "How dare you have another female around MY child?" Yes, the tone of this thought in my mind was brewing with so many emotions. As a now "single parent," we tend to become territorial when it comes to our kids. We become selfish and downright dumbfounded to think we can control the other parent regarding who they bring around the child. Although I didn't "speak my actual thoughts" to my daughter, I surely expressed how I didn't like it and was not going to tolerate it such an arrangement. I called him on the phone while still driving and let him have it. Ignorance from my mouth spewed instantly as he answered the phone. My little messy mind told him a thing or two and tried to let it be known that he will not be doing that again. Just who in the world did I think I was. Who had I become? A jealous divorced woman who thought she could control such things. I was that girl and she was not a pleasant person during moments like this. Confronting him on this only fueled my anger and intensified our horrible communication methods.

These are just a few examples of how throwing out negative words will in the long run, produce negative energy. Negative energy spilled outwardly is generally evidence that something within our hearts is hurting and needs healing. If we're not careful, the negativity will fester into a destructive state that can have damaging effects in the presence of our children. I once read an article titled "Negativity is Noise" and the words resonated with my soul because I knew this to be true. I've never been a negative person overall, but I have certainly had my share of creating my own negative noise. When sharing custody with another parent, communication can be difficult at times. It's inevitable that you won't always agree. We must understand that it's totally okay to disagree. But as adults, if this is an area of struggle, it's best to determine ways to change your participation in negative communication. It doesn't matter if the other person follows suit. We can only be responsible for ourselves and can be responsible in a much more positive manner for our children. A disagreement does not have to be confrontational. As adults, we ought to learn how to use our words to effectively communicate. We do not have to raise our voices or even step out of character to prove a point of view. A friend once shared how she shuts down tones that are not "inside voice" acceptable. She does not allow anyone to raise their voice at her and this is an essential mantra that we all should live by.

I struggled for years with this but eventually made up my mind that I was no longer going to produce negative noise and was not going to be a victim of unnecessary noise. I had to admit and commit. I admitted my own mess and was committed to change it. It was a process but a necessary one because when positive communication does not exist amongst parents, the effects surrounding the child becomes evident. I had to create my own peace and establish boundaries despite the other parent still creating noise. I had to learn that not everything deserves a response, but we all deserve respect. "A lack of boundaries invites a lack of respect. Silence is the best response to a fool" (author unknown). The less you respond to negative noise, the more peaceful your space becomes. For some, being difficult is their nature and we can't change that, therefore, peace should forever remain a priority against problematic people. Sometimes, we have to block, delete, and avoid people or situations that jeopardize our serene space. Narcissists and toxic people will always create noise until "THEY" decide to change. "Narcissists have little interest or empathy in anyone but themselves, and for a child, this can be extremely damaging" (author unknown).

Recently, I read a book authored by a friend called "The Power of Shut Up" by Lisa Dove Washington. I wish this book was around when I became part of this co-parenting relationship. Perhaps, it would've saved me a lot of unnecessary reactions towards negative noise. If you have trouble taming your tongue, I highly recommend you read this book. She touches on how powerful it is to keep quiet and stay silent at times. You will learn lessons of when "To be or not to be Quiet." Once you realize you are part of the problem, seek ways to change. I went to God in total prayer for my inner change. I also prayed for ways to cope with the pessimistic type of person. My prayers in this area never ceased because we can easily digress towards our old ways if someone pushes the right button within you. If you find yourself in need of change, do it. Pray and equip yourself with the knowledge and wisdom of others that have overcome. If you have a personal relationship with God, seek Him for all things and be specific with your prayers, and watch your growth as you receive the peace needed to carry on.

"Dear brothers and sisters, if another believer is overcome by some sin, you who are godly should gently and humbly help that person back onto the right path. And be careful not to fall into the same temptation yourself."
Galatians 6:1

MIRROR CHECK: LESSONS AND LEARNING

What are your takeaways from this chapter? Are you noisy and causing unnecessary strife within your co-parenting relationship? Are you in need of peace when dealing with a difficult person? I encourage you to check your heart, check your motives behind everything you do, and ask yourself what areas need change and growth. Or check yourself to find healthy ways to maintain your peace and sanity. You will continue with a healthier mindset as you proceed in your role as a parent for every child that you're responsible for raising. Pick up a copy of "The Power of Shut Up" by Lisa Dove Washington. Always remain teachable because we're not always right. Once you've mastered this area, you never know when you may need to share it with someone who may also need expansion in this area. Commit to your personal change, find your peaceful place, and cheer on your new-found attributes.

"A woman in harmony with her spirit is like a river flowing. She goes where she will without pretense and arrives at her destination prepared to be herself and only herself." - Maya Angelou

AND THIS MOUNTAIN
SHALL BE MOVED

"You don't have enough faith," Jesus told them. "I tell you the truth, if you had faith even as small as a mustard seed, you could say to this mountain, 'Move from here to there,' and it would move. Nothing would be impossible."
Matthew 17:20 NLT

As we go about our journey in parenting, it's almost inevitable that we'll be faced with many challenges. Challenges that sometimes consume us and become bigger by the day can almost feel like we're being swallowed up by a mountain of darkness. Whether you're a single parent or not, it's a challenging position. As a parent, kids will bring out the best and the worst out of us. When we're met with heavy challenges, it's as though they appear out of nowhere and it's up to us to be the adult and face the challenge and conquer it. Storms will come and often won't make sense at the moment causing all kinds of emotions to rise up within us. We can become so overwhelmed that it allows our thinking to become distorted to a point we begin to believe that a huge mountain in our path is never going to move.

Throughout my co-parenting journey, I personally endured a lot of unnecessary encounters with child's father. Parents don't always have to like each other to get along, but respect should never leave the surface. You set your dislikes to the side to address the child-related issues and handle business. At least, this is how I view how things should be. I have plenty of friends and family that have great co-parenting relationships. So, what was so wrong with making attempts to stay on one accord when it came to parental conversations? Of course, in the beginning years, the adjustment period was to be blamed for our inability to supply a unified foundation. I moved over 100 miles away to be near my family and it prevented opportunities of visitation between my daughter and her father outside of the court orders. Every decision I made regarding anything pertaining to our child does not have to be met with confrontation. Yet, it was so in most cases. Every conversation to discuss child matters is not deserving of disrespect. Yet, it was. Oftentimes, I would reciprocate the same lack of respect, but it wasn't worth it. I made every attempt to resolve a conflict but was never given the same desired outcome. I tolerated and endured too many unacceptable behaviors. Being belittled and called out of my name is not acceptable just because a person disagrees with something. Yet, this was my norm in this relationship. Many times, I allowed situations to harden my heart and cause me to be angry, which eventually made me turn towards darkness to avoid and become numb. Drinking alcohol excessively became my dark hideout for a period of time. I would hang out and run towards those that would comfort me on what my itching ears wanted to hear. Being told "You're a failure of a parent" by my child's father several times was devastating. Here, I was doing all of the heavy work with every angle of school and countless nights of making sure her schoolwork was being completed. I attended teacher conferences and tutoring sessions, not to mention the multiple extracurricular activities I enrolled her in to create a well-rounded child. Yet still, he considered me a failure as a parent. He was always creating problems with no resolution in sight. Why on earth would I allow the spirit of lies to cause me darkness when I was rightly doing all things when it came to providing greatness for this innocent child. Perhaps, because I was absorbing the hurtful things he said and the disrespect that was constantly being thrown my way. It felt like this huge mountain stood between us, and I would allow that mountain to grow every time I was thrown a piece of vindictive madness.

I recall the time when I had taken ill. I had recently had a minor surgery and some complications arose as a result. My doctor had me on heavy narcotics and bed rest. A few days before the next scheduled visitation, I immediately called my child's father to advise that I was unable to meet at the court-ordered drop-off/pickup location, which was about 30 miles away for me and about 60 miles for him. I informed him that he would need to pick her up from our home if he chose to stay on the schedule. He agreed but told me to make sure I was at the drop-off/pickup location on Sunday when his weekend was up. I explained that I would be on bedrest still. He picked her up on Friday and on Sunday, he called and asked where I was since he was waiting at our location.

Now, I already made him quite aware that I was not going to be there and reiterated that once he called. Let's just say that he commenced to yelling, screaming, and ranting for almost 30 minutes about how selfish I was and that I should've arranged for someone else to meet him in my place. Needless to say, I disconnected and he eventually brought her home. I share this story to shed light on how children get caught in the crossfires of "bad parenting." Once our daughter was home, she cried for hours before telling me how afraid she was while in the car with him as he was yelling at me. She was old enough to know what was going on and it hurt her something terribly. These unhealthy encounters appeared as mountains that I had to learn how to climb over and resist retaliation. I knew in these moments that change had to occur because these behaviors were creating an atmosphere of unhealthiness and resentment. Conversations as such would send my blood to a dangerous boil that would affect every aspect of who I was. So, what did I do? I began to pray harder than I'd ever had done. I mustered up the strength to climb over every mountain that stood in my way of parenting. I learned how to not react when provoked. My faith increased. My determination to help our daughter cope grew stronger every day. I sought positive outlets for her. The "I Love Me" girls mentoring program was perfect for her. Her therapist continued to counsel her on ways to embrace the situation without changing her character. I yelled out in my spirit for these mountains to "be thou removed".

By the time our daughter was in high school, she was becoming more devoted to her social time and school activities. She was blossoming and loving life. She was working hard on building a better relationship with her dad.

He would support her by showing up with his family to her dance competitions, fashion shows, and football games where she was performing. At the beginning of her junior year, I entered her into a debutant program that heavily involved both her dad and me. We were cordial towards each other, enough to get through this program that was leading up to the formal cotillion. When spring break of that school year was coming up, the school system first made changes that would cause them to be in school during the break in order to make up for the many snow days that had occurred. She was supposed to spend this particular spring break with her dad. However, the school system decided to retract the original plan to have them in school and granted the entire break back to the students. Yet, our daughter never gave him the update because she didn't want to go with him for the break. Once I realized that she hadn't given him the update, I demanded that she tell him because it wasn't right for her to keep that from him. She told him after the fact, and he was not happy and exploded on her. He then called me and exploded on me for allowing her to lie to him. I listened without retaliation and allowed him to vent his anger, despite the disrespect he was giving me. Later that evening, my daughter walked into my bedroom crying profusely as she handed me her cell phone. The text message that caused her tears was from her father and he said, "You are self-centered-egotistical and selfish just like your mother!!!" Yes, you read that right. These were the exact words. Just like it sounds. Listen, this was just wrong on every level and TOTALLY unacceptable. But like before, clutch your pearls for as long as you need to. But hear me when I say this; when you are a child of God and know your place and your character, you may gasp for air for a few moments. But you best believe I wasn't about to allow this foolishness to manifest in my child's heart and certainly not mine. I talked to her through her tears and spoke these distinctive words. "Your father loves you. Don't you ever forget it. He is hurt that you lied to him and has some unresolved issues attached to him arose, which caused that ignorant statement to rise up and out of his heart." I had to really go hard to explain unconditional love to her on that day and made her understand that her father's attack really didn't have anything to do with her. I had to tell her, "We are moving over this mountain and never looking back." Because she had already experienced her breakthrough in dealing with him through therapy, I was not going to let this to be a setback. She had too many positive resources, supporters, and influencers to bring her to the place of peace she was in. I wasn't ready to let her go away from that peace. I told her to let it hurt. Feel the hurt, but don't you dare stay there. Rise above any foolishness that comes your way. Pray about it and ask God to release you from any negativity attached to that statement. I had to remind her of the following quote. "Sometimes, no matter how nice you are, how kind you are, how caring you are, how loving you are, it just isn't enough for some people." I don't know the author of this quote, but it certainly rings true. Also, I had to remind myself of another quote to avoid contacting him and giving him a piece of my mind; "Never trust your tongue when your heart is bitter or broken. Hush until you're healed!" He never apologized to her. In fact, he told her a few days later that he stands his ground on what he stated in that text. These were all happening at the time my daughter had expressed that she felt like her dad seemed to always focus and hightlight her flaws and rarely gave applause to anything that was near and dear to her. I knew I had to make her understand the importance of believing in herself and to always pray for anyone that invokes hurt towards her; stressing that she must leave all her worries for God to deal with.

A few weeks later, cotillion day arrived, and it was a beautiful affair. Family and friends were near and dear to support this beautiful occasion. Her dad and I escorted her to begin the ball and no one in that room knew the hell she experienced in her heart just weeks prior. I recollect some of the words to gospel artist Kurt Carr's song "For every mountain, you've brought me over, for every trial, you've seen me through." Forgiveness is a powerful thing. No matter the size or magnitude of any mountain we ever face, when you muster up that faith and exercise your prayers to God. Forgive, and that mountain SHALL be moved!

MIRROR CHECK: LESSONS AND LEARNING:

What mountains currently stand before you? Remember, this is a no judgement zone, so there's no need to dwell on the hurting words of this chapter because that mountain can be moved right out of our way. Have you been a victim of hurtfulness attacking our character? I urge you to look beyond the messenger and focus on your character and heart to forgive. Have you ever thrown a mountain at someone out of your own hurt and unresolved issues? It doesn't matter if you threw mountains at a child or to anyone, just apologize, forgive yourself and move away from causing someone hurt. None of us can judge another because no matter how big or how small, we've all had moments of shame where we've caused someone to hurt. Let us learn and grow from it and help somebody face their own mirror.

FROM A FATHER'S PERSPECTIVE:
Stories of men in co-parenting life

Oftentimes, a father will feel slighted somewhat when it comes to his role in raising a child. Whether a man is married, a single father or a stepfather; unfortunately, society does not focus enough on fathers. I felt it necessary to devote an entire chapter to fathers who are doing the darn thing when it comes to parenting. I believe that every father deserves equal praise in comparison to mothers. The role of a father is detrimental to their child. It doesn't matter if the child lives with them full-time or not. There are too many circumstances that could possibly prevent a father from seeing his child on a daily basis, so let's not even focus on the quantity of time. It's the quality of time that a father can get creative with as it could make or break a child. And just like mothers, this same attribute is equally important. A common issue we tend to see is parents competing with each other. There is absolutely no need or any reason for a mother to compete with a father and vice versa. The mistake was that too many times, our daughter was adversely affected by some of his actions, choices, and unkind words. Overall, he's a good father that made some choices and mistakes that horribly affected our daughter. I cannot undermine that. But let's be clear; he is human and makes mistakes like any other person. Unfortunately, some of his mistakes had a detrimental effect on our daughter. I know that he is better than what he felt in those moments.

I have a male family member that was propelled into single fatherhood when his daughter was 3 months old. The mother of the child no longer wished to raise her child and walked away, leaving him to be her sole parent. She actually moved from the east coast to California on the west coast. He raised this beautiful young lady with the support of a mighty village. His parents stepped in when needed and she had a wonderful childhood despite her mother being absent. This family member was doing a phenomenal job by exposing her to different cultures by traveling to various places outside of the country. He is an example of what fatherhood should look like for every child. As his daughter grew into her teen years, she did experience the effects of not having a mother in her life and grew curious in seeking answers at her mother's abandonment. By the time she reached her high school years, unbeknownst to her father, her mother made contact with her. They began communicating on a regular basis and eventually arranged meeting up. This began a whirlwind of events that took place for everyone. The mom ended up manipulating the daughter into making accusations against her dad. Soon after, documents were filed to the court system as the mom now wanted full custody of their daughter and requested to move her to live with her in California. This devastation pulled this young father into a world of gloom and turmoil all in a matter of a few weeks. The mom came with a high-class attorney, finagled the truth about everything and this loving father lost custody of his daughter. She was ordered to move to California to complete her remaining high school years. This totally changed the dynamics of his relationship with his daughter. Although his hurt and devastation overtook him for a brief moment, he never wavered in loving her, communicating with her, and believing that "this too shall pass". This father grew so strong in his faith during the 2-year period while his daughter was away. She not only left her father behind, but an entire family that had been supporting her all of her years. Her grandparents had poured so much into her that they knew that someday she would return. Just as you'd expect, she did, but not before she graduated high school. After traveling over 3000 miles from Washington DC to California to witness his daughter graduate, this father, along with his parents and a few other family members were denied entrance into the graduation venue because the mother would not allow them tickets. The daughter was devastated as she had come to realize that her mother never really had her best interest and was using her to play against a man who had already raised her to be a beautiful, God-fearing young lady. It wasn't long after that graduation that the daughter came to her good senses and returned to where her heart really was manifested. She apologized for her wrongdoings and vowed to get back to where she and her father had always been; a place of unconditional love, compassion, and now forgiveness. This father remained faithful to what he had accomplished in this young lady as he was glad, she had come to her senses. After returning, she admittedly expressed how she knew she was being manipulated by a mother that had no intention of creating a bond with her. It was simply spite, unresolved issues with herself, and guilt from giving her away in the first place. This father and daughter's relationship, though became fragile, repaired and enhanced itself over time. Today, their bond is unbreakable, and the daughter concluded that she needed that experience in order to learn the truth and grow her heart to be bigger than one could imagine.

I have another male family member who has 2 sons with his ex-wife. Their co-parenting relationship is not the greatest, but they both tolerate and are cordial around each other, especially when it comes to their sons. They share equal custody with the boys and have never involved the courts in their family dynamic. He recently posted the following learning opportunity for his youngest on social media and granted permission to share: "A lesson for my son" "My son plays basketball and I sat him out for 2 weeks. Made him go to the games but only to cheer on his team. Had to show him that "you are a student first, not just a student-athlete." Not everyone agreed but I stood up. The principal and teachers wanted him to play. I watched him cry on the bench because he couldn't play, but he still rooted for his teammates. I had to deal with the complaints when I forced him to read and write at home. He improved on his work and behavior and after speaking with his teachers, I let him play yesterday. They lost in the first round of the playoffs. I was so happy to see him be the first one to say "good game" to his opponents and give them fives. He didn't have a great game, but the lessons of accountability are priceless! I smiled when I saw he wore #12. I said you picked my number. His response, "No, that's my favorite number that's on my wall at home. I said I know it's there because I am the one that put it on your wall. This parent's life is no joke, but God saw fit to bless me with two boys that will one day lead a family of their own. No matter what parents; keep fighting to hold your children accountable now before the society holds them accountable later on in life. It may seem like nobody cares but know that what you do or don't do impacts the generations behind you!" What a great example of a father.

I recently met a gentleman at my job who was teaching a training class that I was a part of. Throughout this class, he would periodically mention his kids and would always light up with admiration as he spoke of them. Several times, he would mention his kids' mother in conjunction with whatever story he was telling the class about his children. I later had the opportunity to speak to him and asked for insight on how he was able to maneuver his obvious co-parenting relationship. He spoke freely, stating that his son and daughter were 7 and 9 years old respectively when he got divorced from their mom. The co-parenting agreement was mutual but challenging, and no courts were involved. In the beginning, their personal disagreements would often interfere, and it became tough on the children. She would leverage them to her advantage or ensure that they viewed her as the "good parent." He took the high road and if he didn't have anything good to say about her to them, he said nothing. But they would inform him with some of the things she would say regarding his character. He understood later that anger, hurt, etc. on her part and mind played a huge role. However, he tried to keep the children's viewpoints in mind. He respected the fact that the divorce was tough on her too. It resulted in bitterness and anger most of the time. They both wanted a nuclear family but just didn't get along. The kids were younger, so it was not bad initially because they saw their dad quite often. But as they got older and started understanding better, they experienced some challenges. Negative talk from their mom about dad caused some confusion and trauma. Both kids eventually went to therapy at different times to better understand their feelings. The son started having issues in school. The daughter tried to become a perfectionist as if it was her fault that they got divorced. They clearly wanted all of the family to be together. There were times when the mom would verbalize her anger in front of the kids and her dad usually refrained from arguing in front of them because he didn't want them to see any of their negative actions. But it wasn't always unavoidable. The dad respected her as their mom, and she respected him as their father. He went on to say that he inserted himself into their lives at times when even mom wasn't expecting it; and always made it a point to be a part of their lives - be it plays, trips, sports, etc. He made sure he was always there. His son and daughter are now 22 and 24 and are doing great as individual adults. The advice he gives to anyone going through co-parenting disparities is to understand that all differences between the parents MUST be put aside for the greater good of the kids. Keep adult business out of earshot of the kids. There's plenty of time to discuss, express anger, or other things when the kids aren't around. Also, you have to communicate with each other to effectively plan for all parties involved.

I could write for hours on the number of awesome fathers I've encountered. While writing this chapter, the world experienced the shocking and horrific news regarding the loss of Kobe Bryant, his 13-year-old daughter, Giana, and 7 other lives lost in the tragic helicopter accident. This certainly put things into perspective even for me. Despite the emotional rollercoaster I've experienced with my ex-husband through the years, he is a good father. The fact he remained a consistent presence in the life of our daughter is to be commended. He lives 100 miles away and NEVER missed his weekend schedule visitations. He supported the majority of any event and often traveled with his family to provide extra support. In my opinion, a lot of the chaos that was created on his side often occurred when he felt like he wasn't in control. In no way would I ever excuse or pardon some of the pain that was inflicted because I know that it is common for hurt people to hurt other people when they haven't dealt with unresolved issues around them. I honestly believe that he always had good intentions when reprimanding her, but just never realized the pain and the detrimental effects they inflicted on her. I also believe that I was often the intended target for whatever reason and she often became caught in the crossfire. If I had to do it all over again, I wouldn't change a thing, other than my reactions to some of the chaos. I firmly believe that we both learned a great deal and grew mentally while raising our daughter.

IF IT'S YOURS; OWN IT

One of the things that I try to instill in my daughter is ownership. I do not refer to ownership in terms of material things, but owning your own truth, especially when it comes to the choices we make. When our children are growing up, they often find themselves making excuses for things they've done or blaming others to take the heat off of themselves. They tend to lie or twist the truth to make themselves appear a little better in the situation they are aware they should be admonished. But as a parent, we first must take inventory of ourselves to make sure we are walking in our own truths in order to instill wisdom into the seeds we plant in the heart of a child. It's not an easy thing to do because as a parent, we always think we are somewhat righteous when we give our children rules to follow. Most times, we are, but we still fall short since we are humans. It's equally important to check ourselves to make sure we are walking the same truth we expect our children to emulate. Taking ownership of the choices we make will keep us growing as adults and allow us to avoid making the same mistakes. It will also allow us to walk in truth, and with that comes freedom. Walking in our truth can be painful and uncomfortable, but truth is freedom. How many times have we caught our kids in little white lies as we watch them make attempts to wiggle their way out of what we already know is not the truth, then we recall numerous moments in our own lives where we've faced this same reality?

When teachers contact us about something our child did in class that wasn't a positive thing, we instantly go to the child to hear their side of the story. Most times they deny, blame, or act as though it's something they don't recall doing. As we learn our kids and their behaviors, we can easily see through the words they spew out to plead their case. Even when we confront them with proof or the knowledge that we already have about what occurred, they sometimes continue pleading their case. They often find ways to distract themselves from facing the truth. Distraction, in life alone, is sometimes a coping mechanism that keeps us from fulfilling what we are called to do in certain moments. If we all take full ownership of every choice or decision we make in life, the world would certainly be a better place. Ownership is one of the greatest things to instill in our children. No matter the age, everyone can exceed further in life if we take full ownership of everything we have control of. When you find yourself being distracted by things that serve no purpose, you must endeavor to own it. Learn the lesson and grow from it, and you shall find freedom there.

OWNERSHIP! OWNERSHIP! #OWNYOURSHIT!!!

Distraction!

They come at me without notice, like a bolt of silent
lightning
So heavy yet light enough to disguise that I may not realize
That this is just another hit.
Distractions!
Dying to drive me from my destiny
But I resist and let it flee

Dreams transitioning becoming reality
Of those visions thru faith that I now can see
Though here comes that shadow of a thought
Insignificant to my moment
Yet, clouds surround me taking my eyes off my prize.

Distractions!
Dying to drive me from my destiny
But I must resist and let them flee.

The realization of who you are
Allows my resistance to free me
The thoughts, the chatter, the irrelevance of your subject
Will no longer behold me and strike against my will
Distraction! Do I have your attention?
Distraction! Let me make mention!
You are free to leave

For my destiny is awaiting my arrival
To accept my prize of purpose!

Aleka W. Melson

February 24, 2009©

THE STAR OF THE STORY

The role of a parent is to act as a caregiver in raising a child. When they are babies, we nurture them in a way until they are old enough to start discovering who they are. We guide them and it is our job to protect them and steer them in the direction of success. Although every person has their own definition of success, we just know that we want them to be the very best. Oftentimes, following legacies within a family or being better than anyone in the family has ever been. But how many of us really sit back and allow our children to be the star of their own story? We have dreams and aspirations of particular schools for them to attend and obtain a career we want them to fulfill. But are we so focused on what our desires are that we hinder the mind of the child to develop their own life? If you have many children, you probably know that every child is different. Children form their own unique personalities and create their characters. We can be a bit overbearing when we don't allow a child to become who they are meant to be. It's natural for us to enroll them in activities to give them the freedom to explore various things. When we force them into activities, it can sometimes appear as though we're designing our own person within that child. God forbid if a child goes in the opposite direction of who WE think they should be. Then, we begin to edit every aspect of their life in an attempt to morph them into someone else. We tend to foster them into who "we" are instead of who "they" are. We can't underestimate a child by feeling that they are too young to decide on what "they" want for their life.

I had to learn early on that my child was born and equipped to become whoever she so desired to be. I enrolled her in a prestigious preschool in the hopes that it would give her an early boost. Once she entered primary school, I experimented with different pursuits to determine where she would land with excitement. I enrolled her in Girl Scouts since they are pretty well-rounded and an organization that allows freedom to discover one's innermost self. Outside of scouting, I introduced her to instruments and she chose the clarinet. That didn't last as she outgrew the interest. I mentioned previously that I enrolled her in piano lessons, and she wasn't feeling that either. I realized that I had to let go and let her find her way. In middle school, she joined the modeling team and developed an instant passion for it. She also found her passion for dance once she was in high school. Because she is passionate about these two activities, it advanced her self-esteem and grew her confidence. She found her niche and worked hard at it.

It is vitally important to allow every child the freedom to find themselves. Find what works for them. It doesn't matter if it doesn't align with our dreams and desires. If every generation in your family is a doctor, will you force your child to follow suit? If they protest, will you support that decision? How many times have you heard or seen parents grooming their child to attend a particular college or university from the moment they bounce out of the womb? I'm being a tad bit facetious, yet I've seriously witnessed such things. There is nothing wrong with creating legacies in a family, but not every child will want to shadow their history.

I encourage every parent, whether you're a mother or father. Let your child be who they have been designed and purposed to be. It may not be easy to watch them stumble here and there but support every effort and move along as they grow. You will know when passion permeates their heart. They will shine so brightly when they speak of their calling. Promote every effort and rally around your child at every phase of their growth. I'm a witness at how this makes a difference. When harmony is absent amongst parents, it can have a horrendous effect on a child. But you can counteract those effects. You, as a mother or you as a father, can counteract all of that noise by pouring on your support in all of their endeavors and redirect them towards greatness. Contrary to what many believe, we don't get to write their story. Every child has their own identity, so let us step back and allow them to be the true star of their own story while we guide and provide positive support from every angle. As long as they aren't doing any harm to themselves, to others, or the world, let them be free to choose their lifestyle of choice, whether we agree or disagree. As parents, we're still writing our own stories; so why are we so quick to interfere with the stories of our children? It's okay to step back, and there will be times where it's necessary to "check" them back into reality and in the right direction, especially when they fall by the wayside. Let a child write their own story; their own truth and live in harmony with who they are purposed to be. Plant the necessary seeds and watch them grow into their shine. Invest in the mind of every child that you are blessed to be raising. Help them find their authentic self, and as you do so, you may just end up producing more to your own story as you will learn from their experience. Every child deserves to be the star of their story. Period!

I wrote the following poem for my daughter a week prior to her high school graduation.

SHE

Who is she? She is my everything but really, who is she?
She is this spectacular piece of art designed to shine.
She had to dig thru dust to be clearly defined.
She is this great being that has risen above the noise.
Climbing thru chaos with grace and joyful poise........
Oh, there is more to come and so much more to her story
Writing her own story in order to shine her glory!

CONCLUSION

It is my prayer that you, as the reader, was able to gain some insight from this book when it comes to parenting. Perhaps, none of the stories within this book appeals to you or even applies to you. But it is my hope that the messages shared in this book will save a child from the wrath of pain inflicted by parental chaos, especially if there is disharmony in their home environment. The stories of this book are not meant to disparage the character of anyone, instead, it simply shows the effects chaotic co-parenting can have on a child. If anything written in this book can prevent a family from falling victim to the effects that bad co-parenting can cause, then I am at peace with that. Train up a child in the way they should go and when they are old, they will not depart from it. Be a role model for your child. If you are a mother that's being unfair and not allowing a father to see his child, you are causing chaos and I suggest that you STOP IT. If you are a father that is being unfair and mad about having to pay child support, you are causing disharmony and I suggest that you STOP IT. If you harbor any bitterness, resentment, or any negative feeling towards the parent of your child, acknowledge it and release it. If you are a parent using the court system to spite the other parent, just STOP IT. If you are treating a child unfairly because of unresolved feelings from the other parent, STOP IT. If you are a parent doing anything that is causing your child or ANY child to act out and not enforcing them to be their most authentic self, you should consider counseling for yourself. Utilize every positive resource you can find. Find harmony within yourself if the other parent won't cooperate. Try being creative in establishing healthy ways to direct some of the residual effects of a child caused by parental "mess." Listen to the child. Allow them to express themselves as they have a voice that deserves to be heard. The current generation of children can't be raised like we were. There are too many outside influences within their reach that don't have their best interest at heart. "You cannot raise your children as your parents raised you because your parents raised you for a world that no longer exists." I don't know the author of this quote, but I can assure you that it's a real-life truth.

Some of the things I incorporated into my child's life may not necessarily work for every child. You may have multiple children, yet each of them may or more than likely require something different from parents. Invest and find it. Get creative and keep striving to find something to bring out the excellence in your child. When my daughter was in elementary school, I often wrote little notes of encouragement and placed them inside her notebook or backpack. Somewhere that I knew she would see it. She loved it but eventually outgrew it. I've used all kinds of creative ways to keep her engaged with every stage of life. Even as a 19-year-old young adult, I continue to seek ways to penetrate her heart with love and respect. Shortly after she graduated from high school, I started sending her daily emails to encourage her throughout her day. July 2020 made it a year of sending these daily encouragements and I never missed a day. I made the commitment because I knew she looked forward to receiving them daily as it allowed her to continuously grow. I titled these daily writings, "MORNING TOAST WITH JAM." I had to get creative in order to keep her engaged. "JAM" are her initials, and often what I call her at times. Currently, I am in the process of creating this as a brand.

Some take longer than others when trying to discover themselves. I often wonder why we allow society to put timelines on everything we do. If your child has a game plan for life after high school, then I applaud them. But more than often, our youth are forced into education and giving timelines to complete in 4 years. If they desire this, then it is AWESOME! But as long as they continue to seek and find their niche in life, we may need to step back and allow them to continue to explore. College is not for everyone. That was even a hard pill for me to swallow. I still believe we, as parents, should continue to encourage the educational path and accept when we know it's not the right fight. We must keep pushing a child to develop a plan. No one over the age of 18 should be sitting around doing nothing. We still are required to parent them as they step into every new chapter in life and always letting them know the importance of hard work. Morals and values are everlasting principles that forever need to be instilled in every child. Another big piece of advice is to stop comparing one child to another. I see this way too often and this too can damage a child's self-esteem and self-confidence. Some parents do this with good intentions but it's never cool. Every single child has a unique personality and character. So, please refrain from comparing your child to others. A school principal once stated; "Don't compare your child to others. There's no comparison between the sun and the moon. They shine when it's their time." In my parting words, just as I've continued to reiterate throughout this book, please don't judge any of the people behind the stories. We are all human and probably still on trial for many of the offenses we've projected at some point in this lifetime. If you find that you've exhausted all options to create harmony amongst your co-parenting relationship, create and walk in your own peace and conquer your role as a parent. I once read "A woman that finds peace instead of revenge can never be bothered" This has been one of my greatest lessons and therefore, I have conquered this battle through God's Grace.

"When you finally learn that a person's behavior has more to do with their internal struggle that it ever did with you......you learn GRACE."

AUTHOR UNKNOWN

ABOUT THE AUTHOR

Aleka is a woman on the rise and is chasing after her dreams with her gift in writing as she launches her debut novel. Although this is her first solo book project, in 2019, Aleka was a co-author of a book anthology, Get Out of Your Own Way, Volume 3. Her chapter within that book is titled, Out from The Shade, Into My Shine." She is a sought-after poet as she has spent many years writing poetry led by her spirit that always seemed to touch the heart in a mighty way. She won a poetry contest in 2006 that featured her poem "The Groove" in the stage play "How Hannah Got Her Groove Back" under the direction of Sheritha Bowman. In 2018, she wrote the official poem for the "I Love Me" girls mentoring program located in Ft. Washington, Maryland and is now stepping out on faith to do what God has called her to do. Continuing to flow in her love of writing, Aleka just signed on as a contributing writer for Dove Style Magazine, under founder, Lisa Dove Washington. She fits right into their mission to enlighten, empower, and inspire the world as much as they can.

She was born and raised in the Washington DC, Maryland area and was always a part of some form of activity. In high school, she was part of the marching band flag team and led as captain in her junior and senior years. Her passion for flag twirling led her to become a member of the Spartan Legion Marching Band as a "silkette" (flag team) at Norfolk State University. She is a member of Tau Beta Sigma, National Honorary Band Sorority. During these years, she began writing more about her life experiences and fell more in love with writing, whether it was poetry or short stories. Always desiring to publish a book, she allowed life to get in the way. However, she has grown stronger all through her experiences and is stepping out of her comfort zone, allowing her gift of writing to take her life to another level.

Aleka is currently a member of The Life Center Church in Camp Springs, MD, under the leadership of Jay and Latricia Cameron. She works for CareFirst Blue Cross Blue Shield as a Quality Assurance Analyst. Because of her love to volunteer, she was a Girl Scout Troop leader for 8 years and currently a mentor with the I Love Me girls mentoring program. She even incorporated her love of writing into the mentor program by writing the official poem for this organization in 2018. She also continued her love of flag twirling and became the coach for the Friendly High School marching band flag team, which is also her alma mater. Through her years of leading, coaching, and mentoring experiences, she developed such compassion in working with youth and is now in the beginning stages of launching her own mentoring program for young adult ladies called G.R.A.C.E. "Girls Rising and Creating Evolution." Aleka is the proud mother of a daughter who recently started college with plans to pursue a career in dance and modeling. With her daughters' new chapter in life, her vision is supported by her mom's daily encouragement as she tells her each day to "aim high and fly like a butterfly." These daily encouragements are sent via email to her daughter every day as she created ways to continue to uplift, inspire, and motivate her. She calls them her "Morning Toast With Jam," which has now become her brand that will be shared with the world.

This is the first of many books that this new author is planning as she considers her writing to be "dope" and certainly inspiring. She aspires to become a publisher someday. In her spare time, Aleka enjoys cooking, especially for others, as her meals are always in high demand from friends, family, and coworkers. Don't be surprised if a cookbook is added to her repertoire of writing projects. Just know that this author is on the rise to continue to live out her purpose and passion as she shares her pearls of wisdom with the world.

I LOVE ME

To the person I see looking back at me
My mirrored reflection is all I need to see
She is one lovely sight if I must say so
The beauty in those eyes is that of my own glow
You see, I hold myself to be most true
Your thoughts of me are only for you
My heart speaks to me and everything that I am
My past is just that; as I dance to my own jam.

You see I love me some me
Imperfections and even flaws
Sometimes I must stand still
And take a deep breath and pause
Because this world can be cruel
Will beat me down when I'm trying
But this enlightened journey
It keeps my spirit flying
Each day is different
But this self-love stays intact
If you choose to disagree
There's no need for my clap back.

The same love I have for me
I have it for you also
I am my sister's keeper
And pray that we all grow
Towards this greatness of who we are to be

Finding purpose and feeling free
I know you love you
Just as I love ME!

ALEKA MELSON
©2018